Joe Sixpack's Philly Beer Guide

A Reporter's Notes on the
Best Beer-Drinking City
in America

Don Russell

Camino Books, Inc
Philadelphia

D1044405

Manufactured in the United States of America

1 2 3 4 5 11 10 09 08

Library of Congress Cataloging-in-Publication Data

Russell, Don, 1955-
  Joe Sixpack's Philly beer guide : a reporter's notes on the best beer-drinking city in America / by Don Russell.
    p. cm.
  Includes index.
  ISBN 978-1-933822-10-5 (alk. paper)
  1. Bars (Drinking establishments)--Pennsylvania--Philadelphia--Guidebooks. I. Title.
  TX950.57.P4R87 2008
  647.9509748'1104—dc22   2007051570

Cartoons appearing on pages i, 1, 4, 80, 118, 136, 143, 150, 153, 171, 182 copyright Signe Wilkinson.
Beer labels and brewery logos used by permission from the following: Appalachian Brewing Co., p. 63; Barley Creek Brewing Co., p. 63; Dock Street Brewery, p. 64; Dogfish Head Craft Brewery, pp. 42, 43; Flying Fish Brewing Co., pp. 44, 45; Iron Hill Brewery and Restaurant, p. 70; Lancaster Brewing Co., p. 64; Legacy Brewing Co., p. 65; Lion Brewery, p. 65; River Horse Brewing Co., p. 46; Sly Fox Brewery, pp. 48, 49; Stoudt's Brewing Co., pp. 51, 52; Troegs Brewery, pp. 53, 54, 84; Victory Brewing Co., pp. 55, 56; Weyerbacher Brewing, pp. 57, 58; Yards Brewing Co., pp. 59, 60; Yuengling Brewery, p. 62.
Schmidt's jingle, p. 122, and **Schaefer jingle**, pp. 127, 154, reprinted courtesy the Pabst Brewing Co.

Cover and interior design: Jerilyn Bockorick
Cover photographs by John Taggart | www.johntaggart.com

This book is available at a special discount on bulk purchases for promotional, business, and educational use.

Publisher
Camino Books, Inc.
P.O. Box 59026
Philadelphia, PA 19102

www.caminobooks.com

To my parents, who don't drink beer,
for encouraging me as a son and a writer.
And to Mimi, who tells me she likes a nice bock
every once in a while, for giving me her daughter.

Contents

Acknowledgments

The first Philly bar I ever drank beer in was McGlinchey's in the summer of 1975. I'm almost certain it was **Prior Double Dark**. I want to thank the guy who poured it for me because it was the start of more than 30 years of occasionally crazed beer-drinking fun that ultimately brought me here, to this guidebook. And while I'm at it, here's to every other bartender who ever poured me a cold one, especially Jake, Aimee, Danny, Brendan, Jodi, and Casey. I hope I tipped you well.

They say a newsman lives and dies by his sources, and I wouldn't disagree. I got plenty of help from beer historian Rich Wagner, Don Davidson and the Almrausch Schuhplattlers, wine expert Marnie Old, darts expert George Silberzahn, South Jersey beer gurus Mark Haynie and Gary Monterosso, home-brewing expert and bocce partner George Hummel. Naturally, many of the city's brewers and tavern owners pitched in, especially two who are among Philadelphia's biggest beer advocates: Tom Kehoe of Yards and Tom Peters of Monk's Café.

Other sources of information in this book are The Independence Hall Association, Hickok Sports, RealBeer.com, the *Philadelphia Daily News*, the *Philadelphia Inquirer*, the *New York Times*, BeerHistory.com, the Philosophical Society, PhillyDarts.com, and BeerAdvocate.com.

Also, the following fine books proved to be invaluable resources (I urge you to read them):

▶ *Rum Punch & Revolution: Taverngoing & Public Life in Eighteenth-Century Philadelphia* by Peter Thompson (Univ. of Pa. Press, 1998) is a thorough, very readable account of nation building and carousing with Franklin, Adams, and company.

▶ *Brewed in America: A History of Beer and Ale in the United States* by Stanley Baron (Ayer, 1972) is out of print, but you can find copies on eBay and Amazon. Its chapters on early Philadelphia brewing are illuminating.

▶ *Drinking in America* by Mark Lender and James Martin (Free Press, 1987) is a scholastic look at just how much boozing means to our nation.

I owe a debt to many folks at the Daily News, where Joe Sixpack was born. Former managing editor Brian Toolan let me start writing the column and editors Zack Stalberg and Michael Days allowed me to continue even after they figured out it was about nothing more than beer. Laurie Conrad edits my copy every week and keeps me from making a fool of myself (no easy task). And other staffers (past and present) have encouraged me greatly, including Bob Warner, Ron Avery, Frank Dougherty, Erin Einhorn, Kevin Bevan, and Scott Flander. And here's a toast to the People Paper's original beer guy, Buck the Bartender, and to Bill Conlin, who knows a good fight when he sees one.

Thanks also go to Clare Pelino and Jenny Hatton of Profile PR, who worked tirelessly and kept me full of coffee to get this book into print. And to Bob Wegbreit, who always has another (sometimes great) idea.

I couldn't have created the maps without big-time help from Ramona Smith.

Thanks also to all the folks who took time to name their favorite beers.

The cartoons in this book are the very recognizable work of my colleague and friend, Signe Wilkinson, the Pulitzer Prize–winning editorial cartoonist at the *Daily News*. More than anyone, she "gets" Joe Sixpack.

And thanks to the many, many folks in Philly's craft beer community who've encouraged me over the years, including Andy Musser, Eddie Friedland, Jane Dempsey, Jim Anderson, and Nima Hadian.

Lastly, I can't thank Mrs. Sixpack enough for the many years of humor and love. Theresa Conroy has not only put up with many late hours, weird road trips, and smoky bars; she's the one who named Joe Sixpack. Of course, Theresa isn't looking for thanks—a bottle of Westvleteren 12 will do just fine.

Introduction

Pull up a stool and crack open a cold one. Welcome to Philadelphia, the Best Beer-Drinking City in America.

In Fishtown and Fairmount, South Philly and Center City, this town's neighborhoods are dotted with classic watering holes just waiting to pour you some of the finest beer you've ever tasted.

That's not just some frothy, hometown boasting from a lifelong Philadelphian. It's a professional judgment based on years of careful research. I'm a reporter at the *Philadelphia Daily News*, and they pay me to drink beer—objectively, of course!

For the past 30 years, I've been covering my beat and writing hundreds of stories on deadline, always with a notebook in my hand. It's not only good for remembering what I drank last night; it also makes a perfect beer coaster.

Now, for the first time, I'm sharing these notes with everyone, in *Joe Sixpack's Philly Beer Guide: A Reporter's Notes on the Best Beer-Drinking City in America*. Thumb through these pages and—more importantly—stop in for a draft. I think you'll come to the same conclusion I have: There's no better town in which to enjoy a nice, cold beer.

And, there's no better way to discover and enjoy this city.

Beer, there can be no doubt, defines Philadelphia like nothing else.

We've been crafting it for more than 300 years, since the days of William Penn. We brewed America's first lager. We practically invented porter. Hell, we were already famous for beer when Milwaukee was a cow pasture.

Our forefathers wrote the Declaration of Independence in colonial taverns. Our grandfathers toasted each other with Ortlieb's. We were drinking Yuengling for 45 cents a glass before New York made it trendy (and damn more expensive).

We ain't no pinky-extended wine-sippers; we aren't buzzed on latte. We are blue-collar, hoagie-eating, Eagles-cheering, double-parking, tattoo-wearing, Mummers-strutting beer-drinkers.

Beer is in our DNA.

Just to make that point, I asked a few Philly notables—including some of my favorite bartenders—to share their favorites with you. These guys and gals serve up gallons of suds, so they really know what's best.

And, today, you'll find that we're fortunate to be enjoying some of the finest in the world.

Philadelphia's location on the East Coast means we get the best German lagers and properly conditioned casks of English ale; we drink more Belgian ale than Brussels.

Meanwhile, every American microbrewery either sends its kegs to Philadelphia, or wishes it could—our reputation as a beer–savvy town is second to none.

Of course, we have our own beer to drink. Area brewers like Yard's, Flying Fish, Victory, Dogfish Head, and Stoudt's are producing world-class beer within minutes of our town's tap handles.

Plenty of cities can brag about their beer selection. What distinguishes Philadelphia is the joints that serve all that good beer.

Standard Tap, Monk's, McGlinchey's, Bridgid's, the 700, O'Neal's—these are authentic neighborhood taverns with an honest Philadelphia feel. They're not mass-produced, prepackaged, chain-store vanilla. They're diverse; they have character and history. They are *real*.

Sure, you can enjoy your favorite in your own home, and this guidebook offers you resources to stock your bar. But it won't taste the same unless you get out and order a round in a Philly tavern. Beer drinking, at its best, is a social experience. It's about rubbing elbows, watching a ballgame, relaxing after work, cranking up the juke box, meeting friends, throwing darts, enjoying an affordable meal, and washing it all down with a frosty mug.

Whether you're a tourist or a reg'lar, savoring a beer in a Philadelphia tavern is the single best way to share the spirit and the flavor, the texture and the people, of the City of Brotherly Love.

So, pull up a stool and enjoy a cold one in the Best Beer-Drinking City in America.

Notes

THE BEST PLACE TO DRINK

Is the place where you feel most comfortable. That's what the tavern experience is all about: a solid barstool, a professional bartender, good music, a game of darts, friendly chatter.

For me, a great beer rounds out the entire experience.

Though my bar critiques are entirely subjective, they're based on some serious elbow bending. What I'm looking for isn't necessarily the very best beer on the planet, or the most tap handles in town. Often what draws me to a joint is the mood—mine and the bar's.

But, no matter what, there better be good beer. In this age, if a tavern offers nothing better than BudMillerCoors and other factory lagers—if it can't be bothered to serve even one locally made ale—it's obvious it doesn't really care about beer. So I'm passing.

Bottom line: Use this guide to find the best beer in town. But a great bar—that's a personal choice.

DRAFT BEER

Philly is largely a draft beer town, mainly because of old state liquor laws. It's my experience that draft tends to be fresher than bottles, mostly because it moves so quickly. This is especially true today, as many specialty beers are packaged in smaller one-sixth (sixtel) kegs, meaning they'll kick before they have a chance to go stale.

Most bars serve their beer too cold. Blame it on those tasteless industrial lagers, which are palatable only when consumed at near-freezing temps. Unfortunately, the low temps make it impossible to fully enjoy the flavor and aroma of darker ales. Your only recourse is to avoid chilled mugs and let your pint sit 10 minutes before you drink. See also the section on hand-pumps (p. 98) for locations that serve beer at proper cellar temps.

Not every bar is meticulous about cleaning its lines. If you do run into off-tastes, tell your bartender and you should be offered a replacement at no extra cost.

Some beer, notably sour or wild ale from Belgium, is *supposed* to taste that way. If you're uncertain about an unfamiliar beer, ask for a sample first; most bars will offer one.

BOTTLED BEER

Some bars offer extensive bottle lists. Don't depend on your waitron to know them all; ask for a beer menu.

When selecting, be mindful of bottle size. Many of the finer ales, especially those from Belgium, are bottled in larger 750ml bottles. Be prepared to split them with a mate.

Some bars stock their bottles (and cans) for takeout. An ongoing court dispute over takeout licensing has led many city bars to end this convenience. Don't blame the bartender; complain to your city councilman.

SMOKING

Under the city's Clean Indoor Air Worker Protection Law, smoking is banned in all indoor areas accessible to the public, including restaurants and bars. It's also prohibited at outdoor cafés.

If you need to light up, sorry, you've gotta walk outside. Don't gripe to the bartender; he's probably ducking out for a smoke himself. And don't break the rule because it's him—not you—who's going to get fined.

Private clubs and a handful of bars with limited food sales are eligible for a waiver, but these joints are rare.

Smoking is still legal in suburban bars, though some restaurants and tavern owners ban the practice.

PROMOTE PHILLY BEER

Next time you're in an unfamiliar tavern, ask if there's anything local on tap. If not, ask 'em why not.

No doubt, the answer will be, "Oh, nobody drinks that stuff."

Show them *Joe Sixpack's Philly Beer Guide*, especially the index in the back.

Point out that it already serves a so-called premium (Heineken, Sam Adams, Harp, etc.); why not make that a local micro?

Ask them why they believe they deserve business from a local (you) if they aren't willing to support another local business.

When they finally see the light, remember to return and order that new beer on tap.

MEA CULPA

This guide lists about 450 different taverns, restaurants, breweries, and other great places to drink good beer around Philadelphia. If I forgot to include your favorite joint, please don't yell! Just drop me an email at joe@joesixpack.net.

Invite me over for a cold one. The first one's on me!

Joe Sixpack's
Philly
Beer
Guide

Philadelphia Neighborhood Taverns

N

Bucks Co.

Roosevelt Blvd

Grey Lodge Pub
Mayfair

Harbison
Frankford

95

1

McMenamin's
West Mt. Airy

Germantown
Lincoln Dr.
Allens

Johnny Brenda's
Fishtown

Frankford
Girard

Delaware River

South Phila. Tap Room
Newbold

Passyunk
15th
Mifflin

Montco

611

Broad St.

Germantown Ave.

76

676

95

Dawson St. Pub
Manayunk

Ridge
Dawson
Cresson

30

Delco

Bridgid's
Fairmount

24th
Fairmount

2

CHAPTER 1

Beer Tours

NEIGHBORHOOD TAVERNS

What's the first thing that comes to mind when you think of Philadelphia?

The Liberty Bell and Independence Hall? The Eagles and the Philadelphia Orchestra? Cheesesteaks and hoagies? Rocky Balboa and Ben Franklin? To visitors, these are the icons that define the City of Brotherly Love.

The truth is, they're all cliches.

Anyone who wants to know the true heart of Philadelphia—who wants to experience the best of this town—has to venture out of Center City and into its neighborhoods. There, you will find the best hoagie shop, the coolest boutique, the prettiest street, the funkiest murals, the friendliest people.

Your first step toward discovering it all is at the neighborhood tavern. It is here, along a well-rubbed bar, over a friendly game of darts, with a pint of first-rate beer, that you will meet the locals and discover their city. These are real bars in old buildings that may be a hundred years old. They are not tourist traps and certainly not those phony P.F. McDopey suburban strip mall "eateries" that plague the American landscape. They are filled with reg'lars who know the bartender's first name, and not because he wears a nametag.

Philadelphia's neighborhood taverns are where you'll get a taste of the good and the bad, and, more importantly, a feel for the character of America's best beer–drinking city.

Here are six neighborhood taverns that will give you a decent cross-section of the city, not to mention a fine glass of beer.

BRIDGID'S
▶ Fairmount

Bridgid's: 726 N. 24th St. 215-232-3232.

Web: www.bridgids.com

Getting there:

▶ SEPTA Rt. 48 (15 minutes from Center City) to 24th and Aspen streets, walk 1/2 block south to Perot St.
▶ By car, north on 22nd St., left on Aspen to 24th St.
▶ Philly Phlash to the Art Museum, walk north on 25th St., right on Perot to N. 24th.

Nearby joints: The Bishop's Collar, 2349 Fairmount Ave. 215-765-1616; **Figs**, 3501 Meredith St. 215-978-8497.

Check out: The Philadelphia Museum of Art, which hosts live jazz in the Great Stair Hall on the first Friday night of each month.

Outside McKenna's Tavern at 24th and Brown, a small sign directs women to their own lady's entrance. It's unenforced, of course, but locals—who still call the place "Jumbo's"—hardly want the sign removed. It's an amiable reminder that their home wasn't always a trendy, high-ticket neighborhood.

Fairmount was one of the city's early targets of gentrification, where 25 years ago young urban pioneers shrugged off the street crime and bought up three-story rowhouses for $50,000. Today, they're worth 10 times that.

The payback for those who've stayed (and those just visiting) is a superb selection of neighborhood taverns. Along the tree-lined blocks between the Philadelphia Museum of Art and old Eastern State Penitentiary, you'll find **Aspen**, **Rembrandt's**, **Jack's Firehouse**, **London Grill**, **The Bishop's Collar**, and, most notably, **Bridgid's**.

Inside is a chalkboard menu that changes daily, with almost all of the dishes under $15.

Then there's the beer. This is Philadelphia's original Belgian tavern; it's been serving Chimay since the '80s, when the previous owner entertained guests by running raucous half-price specials just to clean out the fridge. If the splendid tap list doesn't do it for you, take a look in the cooler, where you'll find a **Piraat** or **Affligem Triple**.

Bridgid's beer and the food alone do not make what I believe may be Philadelphia's perfect neighborhood tavern. Instead, it is the bar itself—a small, 15-seat horseshoe that allows patrons to face each other.

And talk.

About sports, about beer, about people, about the city, about their neighborhood.

Hey, did you notice up at Jumbo's they've got white tablecloths now?

DAWSON STREET PUB ▶ Manayunk

Dawson Street Pub: 100 Dawson St. 215-482-5677.

Web: www.dawsonstreetpub.com

Getting there:

▶ SEPTA Rt. 9 bus (25 minutes from Center City) to Manayunk Ave., walk two blocks down Dawson St. to Cresson.

▶ SEPTA R6 regional rail (17 minutes from Center City) to Manayunk station, walk up Ridge Ave. to Terrace St., left to Dawson, left to Cresson.

▶ By car, follow Kelly Drive to Ridge Ave. west, left on Dawson to Cresson.

Nearby joints: Old Eagle Tavern, 177 Markle St. 215-483-5535; **Dairy Land**, 5420 Ridge Ave. 215-482-6806.

Check out: The old Manayunk canal path, just below Main Street, for a quiet stroll after dinner. It links to the well-traveled Valley Forge bike path.

Watching a Saab convertible attempting an illegal U-turn into a 25-cent parking spot so the driver can dash into a pretentious boutique, you begin to see Manayunk as a make-believe tourist destination for young suburbanites who want to experience Philadelphia—clubs, good restaurants, and crowds—without actually crossing City Avenue.

Call it Phillyworld.

A block away—literally on the other side of the tracks (in this case the Cresson Street trestle)—sits another Manayunk. This is the old Manayunk of rowhomes climbing the hill, of Pretzel Park and towering St. John's Church, home of the true Yunkers.

Only, even that's an illusion. Many of the old-timers here have already left, their small rowhouses now filled with college renters. Most of them are short-timers who will never really make Manayunk their home.

Dawson Street Pub takes the best of these many worlds. It is a creaky fixture—a former biker bar—that attracts newcomers with music from familiar locals (Ben Arnold) and serves them honest pints of real ale.

That's *real*, as in the three hand pumps that pull cellar-temperature ale from properly conditioned kegs. You'll almost always find the very best **Yards ESA** and **Victory HopDevil** on line. What you won't find is Budweiser. Owner Dave Wilby banned it in 1995, saying, "That's not the kind of bar I wanted to run."

A comfy couch, a pool table, an outdoor patio, *The Simpsons* on the TV, a Yards—that's the kind of bar this is.

THE GREY LODGE PUB ▶ Mayfair

The Grey Lodge Pub: 6235 Frankford Ave. 215-624-2969.

Web: www.greylodge.com

Getting there:

▶ SEPTA Frankford El to Frankford Transportation Center, transfer to SEPTA bus Rt. 66 to Harbison Ave., walk one block (total 30 minutes from Center City).

▶ By car, I-95 to Aramingo Ave., north to Harbison, right on Frankford.

Nearby joints: Chickie's & Pete's, 4010 Robbins Ave. 215– 338–1190; **Tony's Place**, 6300 Frankford Ave. 215–535–9851.

Check out: The Insectarium, 8046 Frankford Ave., for the largest insect museum in the nation. 215-335-9500.

Crawling up Roosevelt Boulevard, the 10-lane traffic nightmare that traverses Northeast Philly, you have a temptation to write off this vast region as just some suburban wasteland. Strip malls, ugly backlit signs, and ugly brick houses with postage stamp–sized lawns.

Even the people who live here sometimes don't even think of themselves as city dwellers. Back in the '80s, a popular state senator who owned a beer distributorship led an effort to secede from the city.

The movement sputtered largely because the Greater Northeast is not monolithic. Like the rest of the city, it is a place of neighborhoods; Fox Chase, Burholme, Rhawnhurst, Lawncrest—they each have a separate identity.

On Frankford Avenue in a section that can be called either Mayfair or Wissinoming sits the Grey Lodge Pub, indisputably the best beer joint in all of Northeast Philly… and one of the best in America. In 2006, *Esquire* magazine named it one of its 50 best bars in America, a tribute to the quirky inventiveness of its publican, who goes simply by the name of "Scoats."

Its 10 beers on tap are just a start. Grab a pint and head to the dart boards. Back there you'll find a men's room decorated with handmade tiles emblazoned with classic beer quotes. Upstairs there's another bar with comfortable pub seating for dinner. Then there are the events: Friday the Firkinteenth, Groundhog Day Breakfast, Drink-and-Draw, Stout Season, and more.

And it's not just about mindless fun. After 10 years of business, the Grey Lodge Pub has emerged as a neighborhood institution. In 2007, it hosted each of the mayoral candidates in community talks.

It's enough to get you off the Boulevard. Turn right at Harbison Avenue.

JOHNNY BRENDA'S ▶ Fishtown

Johnny Brenda's: 1201 Frankford Ave. 215-739-9684.

Web: www.johnnybrendas.com

Getting there:
- ▶ SEPTA Frankford El (10 minutes from Center City) to Girard Ave., walk one block east.
- ▶ SEPTA Rt. 15 trolley (20 minutes from Philadelphia Zoo) to Frankford Ave.
- ▶ By car, I-95 to Girard Ave., east to Frankford Ave. Or Delaware Ave. to Frankford Ave., north to Girard Ave.

Nearby joints: The Manhattan Room, 15 W. Girard Ave. 215-739-5577; **Canvas Coffee Co.**, 400 E. Girard Ave. 215-425-0524.

Check out: The annual Freddy Adams Sports Tournament, which raises money for scholarships each August.

Before it poured **Philly Pale Ale**, before the kitchen served lamb kabobs, before the stage upstairs showed off indie rock bands like the Big Sleep and Creeping Weeds, before Johnny Brenda's became the hottest neighborhood bar in the city, Johnny Brenda's was...a neighborhood bar called Johnny Brenda's.

Only, that version was a rundown old-man's bar owned by a former boxer named Johnny Imbrenda. They poured you a shot of Schenley's with an Ortlieb's on the back end. The only entertainment was an occasional game of 8-ball.

Johnny Brenda's has changed, and so has Fishtown.

The neighborhood gets its name from its proximity to old docks along the Delaware, and it still has that gritty, hard–working feel to it. The tight homes that hug the sidewalks were built while John Quincy Adams was president. You can still find locals who remember stitching up major league baseballs in their living rooms, for the old George Reach sporting goods company. But where the houses were once filled with workers from the shipyards and the old sugar mill, they increasingly are home to white-collar workers, artists, and young families.

Vestiges of Fishtown's past remain. The kids still play baseball on the cinders at Newt's. The poor still shuffle into the Kensington Soup Society on Crease Street for a lunch of soup and bread. And when the locals die, they are eligible for burial at The Palmer Cemetery at Palmer and Belgrade streets

The newcomers who fill Johnny Brenda's on most nights know little of this history. They are here only in search of a good pint, a well-cooked dinner, some very good music.

And yet, even they are now part of Fishtown's history.

MCMENAMIN'S ▸ West Mt. Airy

McMenamin's Tavern: 7170 Germantown Ave. 215-247-9920.

Getting there:

▸ SEPTA Rt. 23 bus (45 minutes from Center City) to Mt. Airy Ave. R7 regional rail (20 minutes) to Allen Lane, walk two blocks east to Germantown Ave., right two blocks.

▸ By car, travel via Lincoln Drive to Allen Lane, right to Germantown Ave.

Nearby joints: Umbria, 7131 Germantown Ave. 215-242-6470; **North by Northwest**, 7165 Germantown Ave. 215-248-1000.

When it works, racial diversity seems like a dream: people of different colors and social backgrounds happily interacting on equal footing. It is the antithesis of fearful segregation, where people huddle only with their own.

There is no more diverse tavern in Philadelphia than McMenamin's. Black and white and brown, straight and gay and, well, I'm not sure—they sit shoulder to shoulder at this Germantown Avenue tavern, enjoying a hot plate and a Phillies game.

McMenamin's is perfectly reflective of its community, known as the most racially integrated neighborhood in the city. It is the only zip code in America that has maintained a 50-50 racial mix over the past four U.S. Census periods.

It's instructive that this did not happen without some work. When mainly middle-class blacks began to move into the neighborhood in the 1950s, the local religious congregations proclaimed that they would welcome the newcomers, but they would not flee. In the '60s, sympathetic whites made straw purchases of houses from sellers who would not sell to blacks. In the years since, progressive groups have organized social programs to promote diversity.

Likewise, McMenamin's reputation as one of the premier neighborhood taverns in Philadelphia did not happen without work. For most of its 70 years, it was a nondescript joint that you wouldn't go out of your way to visit. Owner P.J. McMenamin did two things to turn that around: He upgraded the kitchen and he began pouring excellent beer. On any given night, you can dine on freshly broiled fish and homemade meatloaf, then wash it down with a **North Coast Red Seal** or a **Triple Karmeleit**.

Mount Airy has its problems, like any other neighborhood. A place like McMenamin's Tavern makes it a lot easier to sort it all out.

SOUTH PHILADELPHIA TAP ROOM
▶ Newbold

South Philadelphia Tap Room: 1509 Mifflin St. 215-271-7787.

Web: www.southphiladelphiataproom.com

Getting there:

▶ SEPTA Broad St. Subway (6 minutes from Center City) to Snyder Ave. Walk two blocks north, left on Mifflin to Hicks.

▶ By car, travel via S. Broad St., right on Moore, left on 15th.

Nearby joints: Hardena, 1754 Hicks St. 215-271-9442; **Ristorante Pesto**, 1915 S. Broad St. 215-336-8380.

Check out: Well-groomed Girard Estate, just a few blocks southwest in the vicinity of 21st and Passyunk. Its handsome Mission-style homes are a contrast to South Philly's blocks of brick rowhomes.

Take a look around Mifflin and Hicks streets, and your first question has gotta be, What the hell is a tavern with a beer list like that (Bell's, Stoudt's, Cochonette) doing in a neighborhood like this (vacant houses, drugs, speakeasies)?

There are beers in the cooler that, before the South Philadelphia Tap Room, had never been served anywhere below Washington Avenue.

The answer is the key to a novel urban development scheme that makes you proud to drink good beer: a tavern whose first-rate tap list is the stimulus for neighborhood rehabilitation.

When owner John Longacre bought the joint, then called Sweeney's, in 2003, his friends told him he was crazy to open a business in a cesspool like this. The section didn't even have a real name, just an indistinct ward in vast South Philly.

But Longacre, a real estate developer, had already taken a look around and realized the neighborhood had almost everything it needed to revive itself: good, solid housing, a dense population, proximity to the subway. The only thing missing was civic involvement.

The taproom would take care of that. As newcomers, attracted by sub-$100,000 rowhouses, stopped in for a cold one, Longacre recruited them for a brand–new community improvement organization. The group still meets regularly inside the tavern, to make plans for the neighborhood's revitalization. Still others hang out late into the night, over a **Troegs Hopback Amber** and a calamari and olive salad, chatting about their new home, about the future.

They even came up with a name: Newbold. It's the former name of Hicks Street, and it's an allusion to the community's spirit.

An idealist would notice it's all very reminiscent of taverns from an earlier period in this town, when American colonists met to discuss and create their new nation.

Over tankards of ale.

THE CONVENTIONEER'S TOUR

If you're in town for business, do yourself a favor: Don't waste your time and expense account on one of those generic chain restaurants that have unfortunately taken root in the vicinity of the Pennsylvania Convention Center. Chili's? The Olive Garden? C'mon, rip off that ID badge and stretch your legs. We're going to walk a couple blocks so you can savor the finest beer in the world at some of Philadelphia's best taverns.

At **Reading Terminal Market**, the well-hidden **Beer Garden** is a welcome refuge from the mad shoppers and wandering tourists. Sadly, you won't find any local beer (except Yuengling) here.

You're better off heading south on 12th Street, past the Marriott (ignore the hotel bar, Champions—it's a dead-end) and the Hard Rock Café. Cross Market Street and duck into the Loews Hotel, where the **SoleFood** restaurant on the first floor has a very comfortable bar-lounge with a nice array of Stoudt's.

Outside, the pace is hectic, so turn right (west) quickly toward **City Hall** (1871). Once the city's tallest building, it is now regarded as an architectural wonder, influenced by the French Second Empire style of the Palais des Tuileries in Paris. That's Billy Penn, not Benjamin Franklin, on top. There are tours inside, but it's the ornate, recently restored exterior that will catch your eye. Proceed south on Juniper Street, a somewhat grim block, past the former Wanamaker's (now Macy's) department store, the first in America. Continue past Chestnut (don't worry, Juniper's safe) to Drury Street, for one of Center City's hidden gems, **McGillin's Old Ale House**. It's the oldest continuously operating bar in the city, attracting the likes of the Marx Brothers, W.C. Fields, Robin Williams, and Tug McGraw since 1860. Excellent local micro selection, including house beers from Stoudt's.

The Conventioneer's Tour — Center City

1 ▶ The Beer Garden. Inside Reading Terminal Market, 12th and Arch sts.

2 ▶ SoleFood. 1200 Market St. (Loews Hotel).

3 ▶ McGillin's Old Ale House.* 1310 Drury St.

4 ▶ Ludwig's Garten.* 1315 Sansom St.

5 ▶ Fergie's Pub. 1214 Sansom St.

6 ▶ Chris' Jazz Café. 1421 Sansom St.

7 ▶ Nodding Head Brewery & Restaurant.* 1516 Sansom St. (second floor).

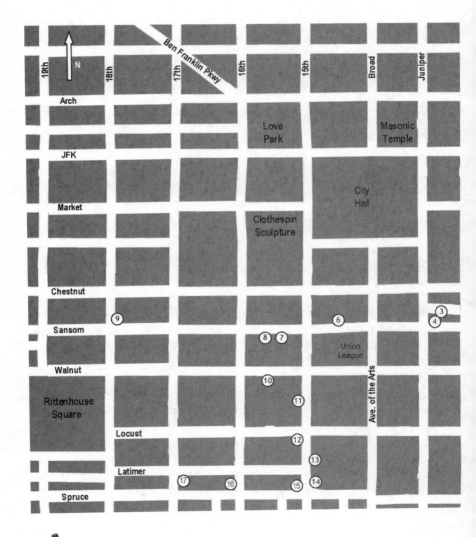

8 ▶ Oscar's Tavern. 1524 Sansom St.
9 ▶ Tria Café.* 123 S. 18th St.
10 ▶ Mahogany on Walnut. 1524 Walnut St. (second floor).
11 ▶ Good Dog Bar & Restaurant. 224 S. 15th St.
12 ▶ Fado. 1500 Locust St.
13 ▶ Latimer Restaurant & Deli. 255 S. 15th St.
14 ▶ McGlinchey's Bar & Grill. 259 S. 15th St.
15 ▶ Fox & Hound. 1501 Spruce St.
16 ▶ Monk's Café.* 264 S. 16th St.
17 ▶ The Black Sheep. 247 S. 17th St.

*Don't miss.

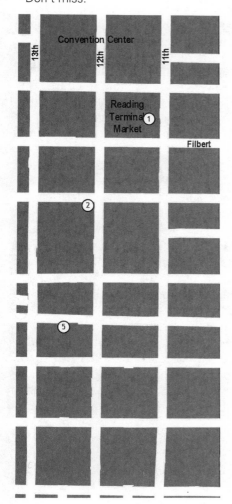

One block south (directly behind McGillin's) is **Ludwig's Garten**, the city's premier German tavern, with impossible-to-find specialties on tap, including **Schneider Aventinus** and **Spaten Optimator**. On Sansom, one half–block to the east, is **Fergie's**, an authentic Irish pub with cask-conditioned ale. Go west, past Broad and 15th, to the city's best

brewpub, **Nodding Head**, on the second floor. If you're lucky, the tart, award-winning **Ich Bin Ein Berliner Weisse** is on tap; don't fret if it's not—you can't go wrong with any of brewer Gordon Grubb's varieties.

Return to 15th, proceed south toward Walnut, the city's better shopping district. Excellent boutiques (Holt's Cigars, Brooks Brothers, Burberry) stretch toward 19th Street, where you'll find **Rittenhouse Square**, a leafy park full of dogs, bench-sitters, and students. The cafés along the east side are pricey, with uneven beer lists. Make your way one block north on 18th Street to **Tria Café**, a classy bistro where you can enjoy exotic cheese and tapas plates paired with an excellent beer (and wine) list.

Return to the east on Sansom Street, past a row of funky boutiques (AIA bookstore with gifts and design books), turn right on 17th, past Walnut. It's here, where the noise subsides, that you begin to discover the reason Center City has so many personable taverns: rowhomes. People actually live in downtown Philadelphia, and after work they hang in the very joints that attract tourists and businessmen in daylight. One example of a classic neighborhood tavern is **The Black Sheep** pub, where locals enjoy a mix of bottled micros and a perfectly poured Guinness with a plate of green curry mussels or braised duck legs.

Outside, follow Latimer Street east or stroll one block further south to Spruce Street, then over to 16th. Either way, you're headed to **Monk's Café**, regarded as one of the best beer destinations in the world. With its two bars (the back bar is cozier), unique tap list (**St. Bernardus 12**, house gueuze from Cantillon), affordable, top-flight tavern menu (mussels and frites, duck salad), and frequent exclusives (the first bar in America to serve draft **Chimay**), Monk's is a treasure.

Head back to your hotel, but along the way visit the **Latimer Deli** on 15th for a sixpack to go. Next door is **McGlinchey's**, a classic, old-time Philly taproom with a decent selection. Further north, on the way to **Good Dog** (young crowd, great jukebox, local drafts), you'll pass Applebee's, the alleged "neighborhood grill and bar." Don't laugh at the unlucky souls going inside. They didn't read this guide.

DON'T MISS

Ludwig's Garten. 1315 Sansom St. 215-985-1525.
www.ludwigsgarten.com. Two bars with spectacular draft
selection, German (gut-busting spaetzle) menu.

McGillin's Old Ale House. 1310 Drury St. 215-735-5562.
www.mcgillins.com. Loud, noisy, and fun downstairs, quiet room
upstairs, good beer everywhere.

Monk's Café. 264 S. 16th St. 215-545-7005. www.monkscafe.com.
Quickly order a draft, then take the time to scan the Beer Bible
for a special bottle.

Nodding Head Brewery & Restaurant. 1516 Sansom St. (second
floor). 215-569-9525. www.noddinghead.com. Small selection,
but every one of the taps is a winner.

Tria Café. 123 S. 18th St. 215-972-8742. A second Tria Café is
now open six blocks east in the Washington Square West
neighborhood, at 12th and Spruce streets. 215–629–9200.
www.triacafe.com. *Tria* refers to the three fermentables: beer,
wine, and cheese. Superb, tight draft and bottle list.

BEER JOINTS

The Black Sheep. 247 S. 17th St. 215-545-9473.
www.theblacksheeppub.com. Attractive Irish pub with excellent
tavern menu and good beer.

Chris' Jazz Café. 1421 Sansom St. 215-568-3131.
www.chrisjazzcafe.com. Stoudt's, Troegs on tap. Live jazz most
nights.

Fado. 1500 Locust St. 215-893-9700. www. fadoirishpub.com. Large
"authentic" Irish pub chain; you probably have one at your local
mall.

Fergie's Pub. 1214 Sansom St. 215-928-8118. The owner's
unpretentious, warm, Irish, and so is the bar.

Fox & Hound Smokehouse and Tavern. 1501 Spruce St. 215-732-
8610. Sports bar with excellent beer, miserable atmosphere.

Good Dog Bar & Restaurant. 224 S. 15th St. 215-985-9600.
www.gooddogbar.com. Great spirit, casual, with pool and darts
upstairs.

Latimer Restaurant & Deli. 255 S. 15th St. 215-545-9244. Greasy
spoon (and I say that as a compliment) with a better-than-
average takeout beer selection.

Mahogany on Walnut. 1524 Walnut St. (second floor). 215-732-3982. www.phillycigarbar.com. Cigar lounge with OK beer, excellent whiskey.

McGlinchey's Bar & Grill. 259 S. 15th St. 215-735-1259. Large, dark horseshoe bar, where the crowd changes by the hour.

Oscar's Tavern. 1524 Sansom St. 215-972-9938. Long bar with Yuengling and not much better. Good, fast food.

ATTRACTIONS

Avenue of the Arts. S. Broad St. from City Hall to Washington Ave. www.avenueofthearts.org. Location of many centers for the performing arts, including the Kimmel Center (Philadelphia Orchestra), Merriam Theater (stage), and the historic Academy of Music (opera, ballet).

City Hall. Broad and Market streets. Tours and info: 215-686-2840. Epic landmark with many sculptures, heroic exterior, and some eerie corners.

Clothespin Sculpture. 15th and Market streets. Reviled when first installed in 1976, the Claes Oldenburg sculpture is now a popular icon, ranking with the Liberty Bell and Rocky as a Philly symbol.

Love Park. 15th Street and JFK Blvd. Former skateboarder paradise with Robert Indiana's iconic sculpture. Cops hassle loiterers with open containers.

Masonic Temple. 1 N. Broad St. www.pagrandlodge.org. A quick, fun tour (especially if you've got a buzz) takes you through incredible meeting rooms representing major architectural periods. Look for Tom Thumb's Masonic apron in the museum.

Reading Terminal Market. 12th and Arch streets. www.readingterminalmarket.org. Bustling downtown farmers' market with fresh food and many places to eat. Disappointing beer garden.

Rittenhouse Square. 18th and Walnut streets. www.rittenhouserow.org. One of Penn's five original squares, it's Center City's toniest park, surrounded by high-rises and cafés.

The Union League. 140 S. Broad St. www.unionleague.com. Established in 1865, this French Renaissance building is home to a patriotic society that was founded to support Abraham Lincoln. Today it is a widely recognized symbol of the city's stodgy past.

Brasserie Perrier. 1619 Walnut St. 215-568-3000. www.brasserieperrier.com. Le Bec Fin's more affordable cousin, with a stylish bar and outdoor seating.

Capogiro Gelato. 119 S. 13th St., 215-351-0900; and 117 S. 20th St., 215-636-9250. www.capogirogelato.com. The perfect dessert after a night of carousing. Try a few samples of the hand-crafted gelato before committing to a delicious (but expensive) dish.

DiBruno Bros. 1730 Chestnut St. 215-665-9220. www.dibruno.com. Cheese and charcuterie, with many specialties available for lunch and light dinner.

El Vez. 121 S. 13th St. 215-928-9800. www.elvezrestaurant.com. Bar and lounge with heavy Mexican pop culture influence (e.g., Day of the Dead, low-rider bikes). Passable drafts with unusual bottled Mexicans (**Casta Wheat**).

The Happy Rooster. 118 S. 16th St. 215-963-9311. www.thehappyrooster.com. Beautiful bar with small dining room. Menu is a bit expensive, but plates are very good.

Marathon Grill. 16th and Sansom, 215-569-3278; and 19th and Spruce, 215-731-0800. www.marathongrill.com. Small, locally owned chain with very affordable menu (available for takeout and delivery). Sansom location has a bar.

Pietro's Coal Oven Pizzeria. 1714 Walnut St. 215-735-8090. www.pietrospizza.com. Local chain with big-time pizza and salads. Very good draft selection for a pizza joint.

The Prime Rib. 1701 Locust St. 215-772-1701. www.theprimerib.com. Everybody's got a favorite steak restaurant; this is mine. Very civilized, with live piano music, older crowd.

Sansom Street Oyster House. 1516 Sansom St. (first floor, below Nodding Head). 215-567-7683. The dining room is overrated, but hang out at the bar for the best fresh oysters and a nice tap list.

SoleFood. 1200 Market St. 215-231-7300. www.solefoodrestaurant.com Inside the Lowes Hotel, good spot for business lunch. Four different Stoudt's on tap.

SHOPPING

AIA Bookstore. 17th and Sansom streets. Excellent design books and very nice gifts.

Black Cat Cigars. 1518 Sansom St. Excellent cigars, many bargains. Old-style shaving accessories.

Goldberg Army-Navy. 1300 Chestnut St. For that French aviator jacket you always wanted. Fun store.

Holt's Cigars. 1522 Walnut St. Huge cigar selection with many expensive smokes and other tobacco specialties. Coffee lounge at the rear.

Home Sweet Homebrew. 2008 Sansom St. Malt, hops, yeast—what else do you need for your own batch?

Macy's. 1300 Market St. Center City's last remaining department store, formerly John Wanamaker's.

Mitchell & Ness Sporting Goods. 1318 Chestnut St. Vintage jerseys and authentic team sportswear.

Pennsylvania Wine & Spirits. 5 N. 12th St. Wine and spirits to go.

Robin's Books. 108 S. 13th St. The city's oldest independent bookstore. Eclectic selection.

Walnut Street. Ever since they started calling it "Rittenhouse Row," the prices went sky high. Still, it doesn't cost anything to look. See Urban Outfitters (1627 Walnut) and Anthropologie (1801 Walnut) for funky women's clothing. Guys, ogle the big screens at Tweeter (1429 Walnut).

TRAVEL ADVISORY

Though Rittenhouse Square is an attractive spot to lay out a blanket and crack open a bottle, think twice. It is heavily patrolled, and cops (not to mention the blue-hairs on park benches) take a dim view of public alcohol consumption, even if it is a $12 Belgian lambic.

THE HISTORY BUFF'S TOUR

You've seen Independence Hall, snapped a shot of the Liberty Bell, and taken a ride on the ducks. Now it's time to experience a bit of history they don't talk about in the official tours. We're talking about beer, the city's first industry, and taverns, the true birthplace of the American Revolution.

From the **Independence Visitors Center**, head north to Arch Street, then east to 5th, the entrance to the **Christ Church Burial Ground** (1719), to pay homage to Philadelphia's first beer aficionado, Benjamin Franklin. He's buried right at the entrance, but if you wander through the quiet plot, you might also stumble across the gravesite of J.H.C. Heineken, Dutch consul at the time of the Constitutional Congress and almost certainly related to the brewing family.

Hang a left at 3rd Street, duck into **Charlie's Pub,** and grab a seat near the front to admire the old buildings across the street. Many of these tightly packed buildings date to the early 1800s, when brewing was one of the active trades in this neighborhood. Before the city expanded to the north and west, this was Brewery Town. Though intriguing galleries and boutiques now occupy the buildings, you can readily imagine a day when burly men would've rolled barrels along the neighborhood's cobblestones.

Continue along Arch beyond 3rd, to the **Besty Ross House,** where Ross is said to have sewn the first flag of the United States, while the aroma of the **Morris Brewery** (Bread and Cherry streets) wafted in from next door. The brewery, one of the city's earliest large businesses, had been making beer for more than 30 years when the Declaration of Independence was signed. Head up quiet Bread Street for a glimpse inside the current building, a condo called The Castings, where you'll see the old brick-and-mortar vaults where beer was cellared.

At the end of Bread, turn right onto Race where you'll get an excellent view of the **Ben Franklin Bridge**. Don't gawk or you'll walk right past one of the better selections of micros and imports (12 taps) in the city, **Race Street Café**. On a cold day, warm up near the stove in this comfortable wood-beamed tavern, and grab a snack from the affordable menu.

On 2nd Street, where you'll see the Blues Brothers and Elvis in front of **Mr. Bar Stool** (a source for bar furniture), turn right and head back to the center of Old City along another bustling block of galleries and boutiques. On the **First Friday** of each month, between October and June, the galleries stay open late and offer free munchies and

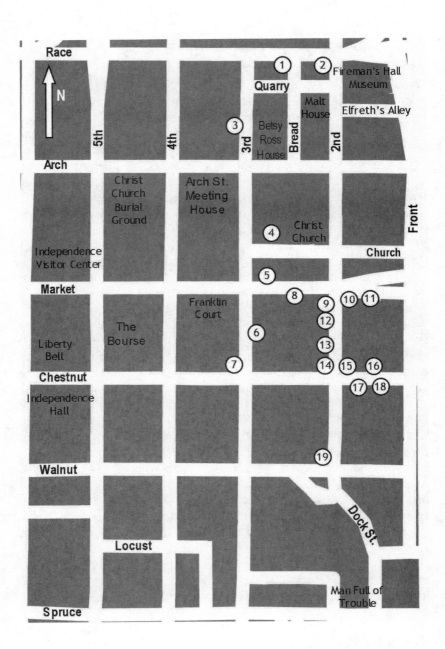

Race

N

Quarry

① ② Fireman's Hall Museum

5th

4th

3rd

Bread

Malt House

2nd

Elfreth's Alley

③

Betsy Ross House

Arch

Christ Church Burial Ground

Arch St. Meeting House

Front

④ Christ Church

Independence Visitor Center

Church

⑤

Market

Franklin Court

⑧

⑨ ⑩ ⑪

⑫

The Bourse

⑥

⑬

Liberty Bell

⑦

⑭ ⑮ ⑯

Chestnut

⑰ ⑱

Independence Hall

⑲

Walnut

Dock St.

Locust

Man Full of Trouble

Spruce

The History Buff's Tour — Old City

1 ▶ **Paddy's Old City Pub.** 228 Race St.
2 ▶ **Race St. Café.** * 208 Race St.
3 ▶ **Charlie's Pub.** 114 N. 3rd St.
4 ▶ **Sugar Mom's.** * 225 Church St.
5 ▶ **Lucy's Hat Shop.** 247 Market St.
6 ▶ **Jager's.** 45 S. 3rd St.
7 ▶ **Society Hill Hotel.** 301 Chestnut St.
8 ▶ **Skinner's Dry Goods.** 226 Market St.
9 ▶ **Nick's Roast Beef.** 16 S. 2nd St.
10 ▶ **The Continental.** 134 Market St.
11 ▶ **Drinker's Tavern.** 124 Market St.
12 ▶ **Brownie's.** * 46 S. 2nd St.
13 ▶ **The Khyber.** * 56 S. 2nd St.
14 ▶ **Rotten Ralph's.** 201 Chestnut St.
15 ▶ **The Plough & the Stars.** 123 Chestnut St.
16 ▶ **Triumph Brewing.** * 117 Chestnut St.
17 ▶ **Eulogy.** * 136 Chestnut St.
18 ▶ **Buffalo Billiards.** 118 Chestnut St.
19 ▶ **City Tavern.** * 138 S. 2nd St.

*Don't miss.

drink. As you pass **Elfreth's Alley** on the left, you'll see the **Malt House** (136 North 2nd Street), a vestige of the old William Massey brewery, which, in the 1870s, was the 11th largest in America.

Turn right past **Christ Church**, once the tallest building in America, and find your way to **Sugar Mom's Church Street Lounge** at the rear of a small parking lot. This is an old sugar refinery; downstairs you'll find a very hip crowd sucking down a fine selection of ales.

One block south, you'll cross Market Street at 3rd, where you'll be in the vicinity of one of the most important taverns in American history, **The Indian King**. In the 1730s, Franklin met here with his intellectual Junto; in the 1750s, the British used it for officer's quarters; and, in the 1770s, colonialists plotted the Revolution here.

Sadly, there is no evidence of the famous tavern, but right around the corner on 2nd Street south of Market, you'll find the strongest concentration of pubs in the city, including the **Khyber**, **Brownie's Pub**, and **Eulogy Belgian Tavern**. On weekend nights this stretch is bumper-to-bumper with limos and trendsetters behind velvet ropes. Visit here at less hectic hours and you'll actually get a beer (and a barstool).

Continue south on 2nd and stop in at the **City Tavern,** a 1976 reconstruction of the original City Tavern, which was built on this location in 1773. That tavern was financed by the city's social elite, who purchased shares to build a facility that would give them a refined place separate from the lower-class rabble and other Joe Sixpacks of the day. Adams and Jefferson met here during the Constitutional Congress, Franklin—now fat and famous—held court in the dining room, and Washington feasted here on his way to his inauguration. Today it's a tourist restaurant that happens to have a very good menu, not to mention **Ales of the Revolution**, brewed by Yards.

March south on 2nd Street, bearing left on Dock Street around Society Hill Towers. On your left you'll see the Sheraton Society Hill, site of **The Blue Anchor Inn**, where, as tradition has it, William Penn ate his first meal in the New World. At Spruce Street, you'll be next to the **Man Full of Trouble**, the only colonial-era tavern still standing in Philadelphia. Unfortunately, the building (1759) is closed to the public, but the fading sign (not original) gives you a taste of Philadelphia's beer-filled past.

DON'T MISS

Brownie's Pub. 46 S. 2nd St. 215-238-1222. Taps an excellent mix of micros, especially stouts, with a game room upstairs.

City Tavern. 138 S. 2nd St. 215-413-1443. www.citytavern.com. Well, yeah, it's expensive, but the menu is superb, and you can't help but suck up the history in this re-creation of one of the most important taverns in American history.

Eulogy Belgian Tavern. 136 Chestnut St. 215-413-1918. www.eulogybar.com. A Belgian-style café with two bars, a superb selection of bottles, its own house beer, and a good tavern menu.

The Khyber. 56 S. 2nd St. 215-238-5888. www.thekhyber.com. The city's first real beer bar (and the second oldest pub in the city, dating to the 1860s). Very good taps and live music.

Race Street Café. 208 Race St. 215-627-6181. Off the beaten track, this comfortable joint has a basic tavern menu and a surprising collection of draft micros and imports.

Sugar Mom's. 225 Church St. 215-925-8219. Once the city's preeminent beer bar, it's lost a step in recent years, but the scene is pleasantly ironic and the selection is still respectable.

Triumph Brewing. 117 Chestnut St. 215–625–0855. This beautifully decorated brewpub is a welcome new addition to the bar scene. Excellent fresh ale with very good food, served on small wooden platters.

BEER JOINTS

Buffalo Billiards. 118 Chestnut St. 215-574-7665. www.buffalobilliards.com. Known mainly for its pool tables and dart boards, but it also happens to have a very good beer selection.

Charlie's Pub. 114 N. 3rd St. 215-627-3354. Very comfortable, attracts mainly neighborhood types.

The Continental. 138 Market St. 215-923-6069. www.continentalmartinibar.com. Martini bar with OK beers and fashion–model waitresses.

Drinker's Tavern. 124 Market St. 215-351-0141. www.drinkers215.com. Your basic Yuengling joint, proudly serving 40s "to make men out of boys."

Jager's. 45 S. 3rd St. 215-592-1613. Hip crowd, lots of taps with mainly marginal brands.

Lucy's Hat Shop. 247 Market St. 215-413-1433. www.lucys215.com. Pub grub with outdoor seating.

Nick's Roast Beef. 16 S. 2nd St. 215-928-9411. Your basic Yuengling joint with very good sandwiches.

Paddy's Old City Pub. 228 Race St. 215-627-3532. Working-man's tavern with better-than-average tap list.

The Plough & the Stars. 123 Chestnut St. 215-733-0300. www.ploughstars.com. One of the better Irish bars in the city, boasts a very good menu and a comfortable atmosphere.

Rotten Ralph's. 201 Chestnut St. 215-925-2440. Loud, young, and beer-soaked.

Skinner's Dry Goods. 226 Market St. 215-922-0522. Good, cheap, and unpretentious.

Society Hill Hotel. 301 Chestnut St. 215-238-6000. www.societyhillhotel.com. Classy room with OK beer, including hard-to-find Straub's on tap.

ATTRACTIONS

Arch Street Meeting House. 320 Arch St. Built in 1804, it's the city's oldest Friends meeting house in use. Very plain but handsome, with no decoration or stained glass. Abolitionist Lucretia Mott was a member.

Betsy Ross House. 239 Arch St. Built in 1740, this is where, as legend has it, the nation's first flag was sewn.

Bourse. 111 S. Independence Mall East. Built in 1893, it once housed the stock exchange, maritime exchange, and grain–trading center.

Christ Church. 2nd and Church streets near Market. Built from 1727 to 1754, this is a majestic landmark where Washington, Jefferson, Franklin and other signers of the Declaration worshipped.

Elfreth's Alley. The nation's oldest street, still occupied by locals. Museum at No. 126.

Fireman's Hall Museum. 147 N. 2nd St. A museum of the earliest days of fire fighting, great for kids.

Independence Hall. 5th and Chestnut streets. Built from 1732 to 1753, it is the most–recognized historic building in America—the birthplace of the United States. The Declaration of Independence was adopted here, and the U.S. Constitution was drafted and signed in its meeting room.

Liberty Bell. Entrance from 6th and Market streets, but you can get a good look from the outside on the Chestnut Street side.

Malt House. 136 N. 2nd Street. Now a condo building, in the 18th century it turned grain into malt, one of the main ingredients of beer.

Man Full of Trouble. 125 Spruce St. In the 18th century, this everyday tavern would've attracted waterfront workers toiling at nearby Dock Creek.

FOOD

Amada. 217 Chestnut St. 215-625-2450. www.amadarestaurant.com. Trendy tapas restaurant with decent drafts. Try the thinly sliced Iberian ham from acorn-fed pigs.

Buddakan. 325 Chestnut St. 215-574-9440. www.buddakan.com. Modern Asian, expensive.

Café Spice. 35 S. 2nd St. 215-627-6273. www.cafespice.com. Indian bistro. Look for **Taj Mahal** in 22-ounce bombers.

Chloe. 232 Arch St. 215-629-2337. www.chloebyob.com. Small, affordable BYO with comfort food.

Cuba Libre. 10 S. 2nd St. 215-627-0666. www.cubalibrerestaurant.com. Looks a lot better than the food itself. Stick with the rum.

Dinardo's Famous Crabs. 312 Race St. 215-238-9595. www.dinardos.com. Old-fashioned seafood joint.

Farmicia. 15 S. 3rd St. 215-627-6274. www.farmiciarestaurant.com. Relaxed, big, sunny windows, OK beer.

Fork Restaurant and Bar. 306 Market St. 215-625-9425. www.forkrestaurant.com. Hip bistro with a good beer list (Troegs, Victory, Atomium).

Franklin Fountain. 116 Market St. 215-627-1899. www.franklinfountain.com. Old-time ice cream parlor.

Old Original Bookbinder's. 125 Walnut St. 215-925-7027. www.bookbinders.biz. Beautiful dining room and bar, but mainly a tourist trap.

Patou. 312 Market St. 215-928-2987. www.patourestaurant.com. Stylish French.

Philadelphia Fish & Co. 207 Chestnut St. 215-625-8605. www.philadelphiafish.com. Good menu, outdoor seating.

Ristorante Panorama. 14 N. Front St. 215-922-7800. www.pennsviewhotel.com. Expensive Italian with very good wine list.

Sassafras Café. 48 S. 2nd St. 215-925-2317. Tin-ceilinged Old City institution with affordable, eclectic menu.

Serrano. 20 S. 2nd St. 215-928-0770. www.tinangel.com. Middle Eastern menu. The Tin Angel upstairs has live music.

Tangerine. 232 Market St. 215-627-5116. www.tangerinerestaurant.com. Spectacular interior, very good Moroccan menu.

SHOPPING

Big Jar. 55 N. 2nd St. Very good used bookstore.

Bonejour. 14 N. 3rd St. Yes, a boutique for your puppy.

Bruges Home. 323 Race St. No Belgian beer, just home furnishings.

Classic Lighting Emporium. 62 N. 2nd St. Massive, sometimes bizarre collection of lighting fixtures.

Foster's Urban Homeware. 124 N. 3rd St. Cool-looking kitchen stuff.

Harry's Smoke Shop. 15 N. 3rd St. Old-time cigar store.

Mr. Bar Stool. 167 N. 2nd St. Full selection of seating for the most important room in your house.

Old City Coffee. 221 Church St. Excellent coffee roasted on site.

Pennsylvania Wine & Spirits. 32 S. 2nd St. For all nonmalt alcohol.

Shane's Candy. 110 Market St. Specialty candy.

TCP Restaurant Supply. 101 N. 2nd St. Browse for unbelievable bargains for your kitchen and bar.

WEB SOURCES

Galleries: www.oldcityarts.org.
History: www.ushistory.org.
Shops, restaurants: www.oldcitydistrict.org.

TRAVEL ADVISORY

Grab a large bottle at Mulberry Market (236 Arch Street) and some aged Gouda at **Old City Cheese** (160 N. 3rd), then head over to Franklin Square (6th and Race) for a quiet (daylight only) picnic. Keep the bottle in brown paper and sip from cups and nobody will bother you here.

LEG-STRETCHERS

Bouncing from one joint to the next without getting behind the wheel is one of the benefits of drinking in the city. Here are two excellent beer-focused bar-hopping destinations for those who don't mind a little exercise.

ART MUSEUM

Take SEPTA bus routes 7, 32, 38, 43, 48, or Philly Phlash to the Philadelphia Museum of Art. Cross Kelly Drive to 25th Street, go north, then right on Fairmount Avenue for a beer-filled neighborhood stroll in the shadow of the old Eastern State Penitentiary:

The Bishop's Collar. 2349 Fairmount Ave. 215-765-1616. www.thebishopscollar.citysearch.com. Fun, noisy.
London Grill. 2301 Fairmount Ave. 215-978-4545. www.londongrill.com. Brit pub.
Jack's Firehouse. 2130 Fairmount Ave. 215-232-9000. www.jacksfirehouse.com. American gourmet.

Turn north on 23rd to:

Rembrandt's Restaurant and Bar. 741 N. 23rd St. 215-763-2228. www.rembrandts.com. Upscale tavern.

Then left on Aspen, left on 24th to Perot:

Bridgid's. 726 North 24th St. 215-232-3232. www.bridgids.com. Neighborhood Belgian.

Then back to 25th to:

Aspen Restaurant & Bar. 747 N. 25th St. 215-232-7736. www.theaspenrestaurant.com. Cozy.

Return south on 25th to the Art Museum.

NORTHERN LIBERTIES

Take the Frankford El to Girard Avenue, and if you need an immediate drink, head east one block to **Johnny Brenda's** (1201 Frankford Avenue) for a draft. Or get the driest leg of your walk out of the way by heading west, up Girard to 2nd Street, then south to one of the best stretches of beer and food in the city:

Deuce Restaurant & Bar. 1040 N. 2nd St. 215-413-3822.
   www.deucerestaurant.com. Affordable upscale.
Bar Ferdinand. 1030 N. 2nd St. 215-923-1313.
   www.barferdinand.com. Tapas.
North Bowl. 909 N. 2nd St. 215-238-2695.
   www.northbowlphilly.com. Bowling.
Standard Tap. 901 N. 2nd St. 215-238-0630. www.standardtap.com.
   Gastropub.
The Foodery. 837 N. 2nd St. 215-238-6077. www.fooderybeer.com.
   Takeout beer.

Turn west on Poplar, then south on 3rd to:

Ortlieb's Jazzhaus. 847 N. 3rd St. 215-922-1035.
   www.ortliebsjazzhaus.com. Live music.
North 3rd. 801 N. 3rd St. 215-413-3666. www.norththird.com.
   Good food.
Abbaye. 637 N. 3rd St. 215-627-6711. Belgian.

Turn left on Fairmount to 2nd.

700. 700 N. 2nd St. 215-413-3181. Bike messengers and neighbors
   who lived here before it all got so trendy.
Liberties. 705 N. 2nd St. 215-238-0660. www.libertiesrestaurant.com.
   Older crowd.
Druid's Keep. 149 Brown St. 215-413-0455. Young urban pioneers.

Continue south on 2nd to Spring Garden, where you can either hop back onto the El or get totally shit-faced at:

McFadden's. 461 N. 3rd St. 215-928-0630.
   www.mcfaddensphilly.com. Loud Irish.
Finnigan's Wake. 537 N. 3rd St. 215-574-9317. www.finnigans.com.
   Crowded Irish.

AROUND TOWN

Philly is a big place with lots of other nooks to explore. You don't even need a guidebook—just plunk yourself onto a barstool in one of these joints (note all–capped venues especially), order a cold one, and ask a local.

CENTER CITY EAST

Caribou Café. 1126 Walnut St. 215-625-9535.
Dirty Frank's Bar. 347 S. 13th St. 215-732-5010.
Doc Watson's. 216 S. 11th St. 215-922-3427.
Irish Pub. 1123 Walnut St. 215-925-3311. www.irishpubphilly.com.
Las Vegas Lounge. 704 Chestnut St. 215-592-9533.
    www.lasvegaslounge.com.
Locust Bar. 235 S. 10th St. 215-925-2191.
Mace's Crossing Pub. 1714 Cherry St. 215-564-5203.
MORIARTY'S. 1116 Walnut St. 215-627-7676.
Vintage. 129 S. 13th St. 215-922-3095. www.13thstreetwinebar.com.

CENTER CITY WEST

1912 Bar. 1912 Arch St. 215-564-1131.
Bar Noir. 112 S. 18th St. 215-569-1160. www.barnoir215.com.
The Bards. 2013 Walnut St. 215-569-9585. www.bardsirishbar.com.
Bob and Barbara's Lounge. 1509 South St. 215-545-4511.
Brasserie Perrier. 1619 Walnut St. 215-568-3000.
    www.brasserieperrier.com.
Chaucer's Tabard Inn. 1946 Lombard St. 215-985-9663.
Cherry Street Tavern. 129 N. 22nd St. 215-561-5683.
Continental Midtown. 1801 Chestnut St. 215-567-1800.
    www.continentalmidtown.com.
Devil's Alley. 1907 Chestnut St. 215-751-0707.
    www.devilsalleybarandgrill.com.
DOOBIES. 2201 Lombard St. 215-546-0316.
Drinker's Pub. 1903 Chestnut St. 215-564-0914.
    www.drinkerspub215.com.
Irish Pub. 2007 Walnut St. 215-568-5603. www.irishpubphilly.com.
JOSE PISTOLA'S. 263 S. 15th St. 215–545–4101.
    www.josepistolas.com.
Loie Brasserie & Bar. 128 S. 19th St. 215-568-0808.
    www.loie215.com.

Noche Lounge. 1901 Chestnut St. 215-568-0551.
www.noche215.com.

Public House. 2 Logan Sq. 215-587-9040.

Roosevelt's Pub. 2222 Walnut St. 215-569-8879.

TANGIER. 1801 Lombard St. 215-732-5006.

TEN STONE. 2063 South St. 215-735-9939. www.tenstone.com.

Tir na Nog Irish Bar & Grill. 1600 Arch St. 215-514-1700.
www.tirnanogphilly.com.

Tritone. 1508 South St. 215-545-0475. www.tritonebar.com.

Twenty21. 2005 Market St. 215-851-6270. www.twenty-21.com.

CHESTNUT HILL

McNally's Tavern. 8634 Germantown Ave. 215-247-9736.
www.mcnallystavern.com.

Mermaid Inn. 7673 Germantown Ave. 215-247-9797.
www.themermaidinn.net.

MANAYUNK/EAST FALLS

FLAT ROCK SALOON. 4301 Main St., 215-483-3722.

OLD EAGLE TAVERN. 177 Markle St. 215-483-5535.

Thumper's East Falls Grill. 3521 Bowman St. 215-981-4975.
www.theeastfallsgrill.com.

Ugly Moose. 443 Shurs Lane. 215-482-BREW.
www.theuglymoose.com.

UNION JACK'S PUB. 4801 Umbria St. 215-482-8980.

NORTH PHILLY

(including Northern Liberties, Fairmount, Spring Garden)

THE BELGIAN CAFÉ. 2047 Green St. 215–235–3500.

The Draught Horse. 1431 Cecil B. Moore Ave. 215-235-1010.
www.draughthorse.com.

The Fire. 412 W. Girard Ave. 267-671-9298.

The Green Room. 1940 Green St. 215-241-6776.

Kelliann's. 1549 Spring Garden St. 215-563-6990.

Makers Local. 501 N. 13th St. 215–627–0731.

McCrossen's Tavern. 529 N. 20th St. 215-854-0923.
www.mcrossens.com.

North Star Bar. 2639 Poplar St. 215-684-0808.
www.northstarbar.com.

Philadelphila Bar & Grill. 412 W. Girard Ave. 215-671-9298.
Rose Tattoo Café. 1847 Callowhill St. 215-569-8939.
www.rosetattoocafe.com.
St. Stephen's Green. 1701 Green St. 215–769–5000.
Urban Saloon. 2120 Fairmount Ave. 215–808–0348.
Westy's. 1440 Callowhill St. 215-563-6134.

GREATER NORTHEAST

Blue Ox Bistro. 7980 Oxford Ave. 215-728-9440.
www.blueoxbistro.com.
Chickie's & Pete's. 11000 Roosevelt Blvd, Bustleton. 215-856-9890.
www.chickiesandpetes.com.
Three Monkeys Café. 9645 James St. 215-637-6665.
www.3monkeyscafe.com.

SOUTH PHILLY

(including Bella Vista, Queen Village, Point Breeze)

12 Steps Down. 831 Christian St. 215-238-0379.
1601 Bar. 1601 S. 10th St. 215-218-3840.
Chickie's & Pete's. 1526 Packer Ave. 215-218-0500.
www.chickiesandpetes.com.
Chick's Café and Wine Bar. 614 S. 7th St. 215–625–3700.
www.chickscafe.com.
FOR PETE'S SAKE. 900 S. Front St. 215-462-2230.
www.forpetesakepub.com.
Friendly Lounge. 1039 S. 8th St. 215-627-9798.
GRACE TAVERN. 2229 Gray's Ferry Ave. 215-893-9580.
Latest Dish. 613 S. 4th St. 215-629-0565. www.latestdish.com.
New Wave Café. 784 S. 3rd. St. 215-922-8484.
www.newwavecafe.com.
Penn's Port Pub. 1920 S. Delaware Ave. 215-336-7003.
www.pennsportpub.com.
Pub on Passyunk East. 1501 E. Passyunk Ave. 215-755-5125.
ROYAL TAVERN. 937 E. Passyunk Ave. 215-389-6694.
www.royaltavern.com.
The Sidecar Bar & Grille. 2201 Christian St. 215-732-3729.
www.thesidecarbar.com.

SOUTH STREET AREA

Ansill. 627 S. 3rd St. 215-627-2485. www.ansillfoodandwine.com.

The Artful Dodger. 400 S. 2nd. St. 215-922-1790.
www.artfuldodgerphilly.com.

Bridget Foy's. 200 South St. 215-922-1813. www.bridgetfoys.com.

Cheers to You. 430 South St. 215-923-8780.

Dark Horse Pub. 421 S. 2nd St. 215-928-9307.
www.darkhorsepub.com.

THE DIVE. 947 E. Passyunk Ave. 215-465-5505.

Downey's Restaurant. 526 S. Front St. 215-625-9500.
www.downeysrestaurant.com.

O'NEAL'S. 611 S. 3rd St. 215-574-9495. www.onealspub.com.

Southwark. 701 S. 4th St. 215-238-1888.

Tori's Brick House. 626 S. Front St. 215-627-4866.
www.torisbrickhouse.com.

WEST PHILLY

Bridgewater's Pub. 2951 Market St., 30th Street Station. 215-387-4787.

Cavanaugh's Restaurant. 119 S. 39th St. 215-386-4889.
www.cavanaughsrestaurant.com.

Kelliann's. 4333 Spruce St. 215-222-4188.

MAD MEX. 3401 Walnut St. 215-382-2221. www.madmex.com.

New Deck Tavern. 3408 Sansom St. 215-386-4600.
www.newdecktavern.com.

Slainte. 30th and Market sts. 215–386–4600. www.slaintephilly.com.

Smokey Joe's Tavern. 210 S. 40th St. 215-222-0770.
www.smokeyjoesbar.com.

WHITE DOG CAFÉ. 3420 Sansom St. 215-386-9224.
www.whitedog.com.

SUBURBAN SURVIVAL GUIDE

Cleaner streets, lower taxes, superior schools, more jobs, fewer psy-chopaths, greener grass, bigger malls, easier parking, safer neighbor-hoods—the suburbs can have it all. Because the city has better beer.

I wrote that 10 years ago, before the suburbs finally discovered that "light" is not a required adjective when describing beer. Today, the suburbs have more brewpubs than the city, and they're sprouting a number of top-rate beer bars.

Yes, it is still plagued with fun-and-food "eateries" that serve moz-zarella sticks and have an unfortunate tendency to allow children to sit at the bar. It is very easy to get lost amid the cul de sacs with only strip malls in sight.

The next time you venture beyond City Avenue, bring along this handy survival guide to beer bars in the sticks.

▶ **You're visiting your brother-in-law at Graterford Prison.**
Ortino's Northside. 1355 Gravel Pike, Zieglersville. 610-287-8333. www. ortinos.com. Use fake gun carved from bar of soap to get past guards, take Rt. 29 north, 9 minutes.

▶ **Your partner insists on spending the afternoon in New Hope.**
Havana. 105 S. Main St., New Hope. 215-862-5501. www. havananewhope.com. Watch him/her scour the boutiques from your perch at the outdoor bar.

▶ **Your husband, the history buff, is in a historical reenactment at Valley Forge Park.**
Iron Hill Brewery. 130 E. Bridge St., Phoenixville. 610.983.9333. www.ironhillbrewery.com. Toss that tri-cornered hat in the trash, go west on Rt. 23, right on Starr St., left on Bridge. 5 minutes.

▶ **Your out-of-town guests insisted on going to Amish country.**
Lancaster Dispensing Co., 33 N. Market St., Lancaster. 717-299-2444. www.dispensingco.com. Pass that buggy on Rt. 222 and head into the center of town, near W. King Street.

▶ **You just got out of rehab at Eagleville Hospital.**
Brother Paul's. 3300 Ridge Ave., Eagleville. 610-539-3909. www.brotherpauls.com. Chuck the methadone, go north on Eagleville Rd. to Ridge, 1 minute.

► **You thought there were actual peddlers at Peddler's Village.**

Porterhouse Restaurant & Brew Pub. 5775 Lower York Rd., Lahaska. 215-794-9373. www.porterhousepub.com. Rip up your credit card and cross the street, 1 minute.

► **You're dropping off your smartass kid at college.**

The Alchemist & Barrister. 28 Witherspoon St., Princeton, N.J. 609-925-5555. www.alchemistandbarrister.com. Make the check out to Princeton University, then head out on Nassau St., turn onto Witherspoon, 5-minute walk.

► **You're dropping off your slacker kid at college.**

Iron Hill Brewery. 3 W. Gay St., West Chester. 610-738-9600. www.ironhillbrewery.com. While he's unpacking his Game Boy at the West Chester University dorms, head up High St., to Gay, 2 minutes.

► **You're dropping off your dumbass kid at college.**

Blue Horse Inn. 602 Skippack Pike, Blue Bell. 215-641-0512. www.thebluehorse.com. It's too late to hire an SAT tutor, exit Montgomery County Community College on Dekalb Pike, left on Skippack Pike, 5 minutes.

► **You thought you could bet the trifecta at the Devon Horse Show.**

John Harvard's Brew House. 629 W. Lancaster Ave., Wayne. 610-687-6565. www.johnharvards.com. Giddy-up, equestrian boy, and ride east on Lancaster Ave., 2 minutes.

► **You're taking your mother to Longwood Gardens.**

Half Moon Restaurant & Saloon. 108 W. State St., Kennett Square. 610-444-7232. www.halfmoonrestaurant.com. Cut her a nice bouquet, then hightail it on Baltimore Pike south to State St., 5 minutes.

► **Your kids want to go to Sesame Place.**

Hulmeville Inn. 4 Trenton Rd., Hulmeville. 215-750-6893. www.hulmevilleinn.com. Tell the brats to stop crying, head west on Lincoln Highway, left on Bellevue, left on Neshaminy to Trenton Ave., 10 minutes.

► **You're caught in a traffic jam on the Blue Route.**

EXIT 3. Media/Swarthmore.

Quotations. 37 E. State St., Media. 610-627-2515. Baltimore Pike west, right on Monroe St. to State.

EXIT 9. Broomall.

Westgate Pub. 1021 West Chester Pike, Havertown. 610-446-3030. www.westgatepub.com. East on Rt. 3 (West Chester Pike).

EXIT 13. St. Davids.

Teresa's Next Door. 126 N. Wayne Ave., Wayne. 610–293–0119. West on Rt. 30, right on N. Wayne.

EXIT 16. Conshohocken.

Flanigan's Boathouse. 113 Fayette St. 610-828-2628. www.flanigansboathouse.com. Right onto Matsonford Road, continue over bridge to Fayette.

EXIT 19. Germantown Pike.

Ye Olde Ale House. 405 Germantown Pike, Lafayette Hill. 610-825-2469. Right on Germantown Ave., east.

► **You just had to hear David Bromberg again at the Keswick Theater.**

G.G. Brewers. 282 Keswick Rd., Glenside. 215-887-0809. Pretend you're heading out for a doober, cross the street, 60 seconds.

► **You had a misplaced urge to smell the fresh air at Nock-amixon State Park.**

Revivals. 4 S. Ridge Rd., Perkasie. 215-258-3463. www.revivalsrestaurant.com. Put down that damn fishing pole, Opie, and take Dublin Pike south to Ridge Rd., right into Perkasie, 10 minutes.

► **You really needed a pair of size 56 overalls at Zern's Farmer's Market.**

Union Jack's Inn on the Manatawny. 546 Manatawny Road, Boyertown. 610-689-0189. Don't forget to grab some shoo-fly pie, follow Rt. 73 west, bear left on Toll House Rd., left on Manatawny Rd., 15 minutes.

► **Your wife dragged you to the mall.**

PENNSYLVANIA

Exton

Inside: **Houlihan's**, near Boscov's. 610-524-9500.
Outside: **The Drafting Room.** 634 N. Pottstown Pike (Rt. 100), Exton. 610-363-0521. www.draftingroom.com.

Granite Run

Inside: **Ruby Tuesday,** near Boscov's. 610-891-6711.
Outside: **Iron Hill Brewery,** 30 E. State St., Media. 610-627-9000.

King of Prussia

Inside: **Rock Bottom Brewery,** near Sears. 610-230-2739. www.rockbottom.com.
Outside: Don't bother; the traffic's a mess.

Montgomery

Inside: **T.G.I. Friday's,** located in the parking lot. 215-412-4221.
Outside: **Wingwalker Pub.** 249 Bethlehem Pike, Colmar. 215–822–6610. www.innflightrestaurants.com.

Neshaminy

Inside: **Manny Brown's,** near theater. 215-357-9242.
Outside: **Newportville Inn,** 4120 Lower Rd., Newportville. 215-785-6090. www.newportvilleinn.net.

Oxford Valley

Inside: **Charlie Brown's,** located in the parking lot at Middletown Blvd. 215-757-8830.
Outside: **Isaac Newton's.** 18 S. State St., Newtown. 215-860-5100. www.isaacnewtons.com.

Plymouth Meeting

Inside: **Bertucci's,** near Boscov's. 610-397-0650.
Outside: **Capone's.** 224 W. Germantown Pike. 610-279-4748.

Willow Grove Park

Inside: **T.G.I. Friday's,** near Express. 215-657-1597.
Outside: **Otto's Brauhaus.** 233 Easton Rd., Horsham. 215-675-1864.

NEW JERSEY

Cherry Hill

Inside: **Houlihan's,** next to The Gap. 856-662-9300.
Outside: **P.J. Whelihan's Pub,** 1854 E. Marlton Pike, Cherry Hill. 856-424-8844. www.pjspub.com.

Deptford

Inside: **Ruby Tuesday,** near Sears. 856-845-3330.
Outside: **Cap'n Cats Clam Bar & Tavern.** 1416 Crown Point Rd., Westville. 856-853-1844.

Echelon

Inside: No alcohol, BYO flask.
Outside: **Main Street Pub.** 2012 Main St., Voorhees. 856-424-8770.

Moorestown

Inside: You're S.O.L., guy. Moorestown is dry.
Outside: **P.J. Whelihan's Pub.** 338 S. Lenola Rd., Maple Shade. 856-234-2345.

MORE SUBURBAN JOINTS

If you don't have any idea why you're in the 'burbs, maybe you're just lost. Don't fear; there's sure to be a decent beer joint just around the corner. And believe it or not, some are worth a special trip (see all-capped venues).

BERKS COUNTY

Flying Dog. 7408 Boyertown Pike, Earlville. 610-656-7509.
Stopper's. 6421 Perkiomen Ave., Birdsboro. 610-582-8911.
UGLY OYSTER DRAFTHAUS. 21 S. 5th St., Reading. 610-373-6791. www.theuglyoyster.com.

BUCKS COUNTY

BETHAYRES TAVERN. 2231 Huntingdon Pike, Huntingdon Valley. 215-947-9729. www.bethayrestavern.com.
BRICK HOTEL. 1 E. Washington Ave., Newtown. 215-860-8313. www.brickhotel.com.
Cross Keys Pub. 3710 N. Easton Rd., Doylestown. 215-345-8020.
JUST SPORTS. 600 New Rodgers Rd., Bristol. 215-781-9556. www.justsportsbarandgrill.com.

MESQUITO GRILLE. 128 W. State St., Doylestown. 215-230-7427.

Piper Tavern. Rt. 413 and Dark Hollow Rd., Pipersville. 215-766-7100. www.pipertavern.com.

SPINNERSTOWN HOTEL RESTAURANT. 2195 Spinnerstown Rd., Spinnerstown. 215-536-7242. www.spinnerstownhotel.com.

Tony's Place Bar & Grill. 1297 Greeley Ave., Warminster. 215-675-7275.

WASHINGTON HOUSE. 136 N. Main St., Sellersville. 215-257-3000. www.washingtonhouse.com.

CHESTER COUNTY

Brickside Grille. 540 Wellington Sq., Exton. 610-321-1600. www.bricksidegrille.com.

Casey's Olde Ale House. 543 Lancaster Ave., Berwyn. 610-644-5086.

FLANIGAN'S BOATHOUSE. 6 Great Valley Parkway, Malvern. 610-251-0207. www.flanboathouse.com.

FLYING PIG SALOON. 121 E. King St., Malvern. 610-578-9208.

Nectar. 1091 Lancaster Ave., Berwyn. 610-725-9000. www.tastenectar.com.

Ryan's Pub. 124 W. Gay St., West Chester. 610-344-3934. www.ryans-pub.com.

T.J.'S EVERYDAY. 35 Paoli Plaza, Paoli. 610-725-0100. www.tjseveryday.com.

Wayne Beef & Ale. 232 W. Wayne Ave., Wayne. 610-688-2337. www.waynebeefandale.com.

DELAWARE COUNTY

Brownie's Pub. 26 Garrett Road, Upper Darby. 610-352-3290.

FIREWATERS. 1119 Baltimore Pike, Glen Mills. 610-459-9959.

Oakmont National. 31 Eagle Rd., Havertown. 610-789-4000. www.oakmontnationalpub.com.

Riddle Ale House. 1073 W. Baltimore Pike, Media. 610-566-9984. www.riddlealehouse.net.

MONTGOMERY COUNTY

All Star Café. 2485 Swamp Pike, Gilbertsville. 610-327-9192.

The Austrian Village. 321 Huntingdon Pike, Rockledge. 215–663–9902.

Blue Bell Inn. 601 Skippack Pike, Blue Bell. 215-646-2010. www.bluebellinn.com.

Blue Comet. 106 S. Easton Road, Glenside. 215-922-8157. www.bluecometbarandgrill.com.

Blue Dog Pub. 950 S. Valley Forge Rd., Lansdale. 215-368-6620.

Brittingham's Irish Pub. 540 E. Germantown Pike, Lafayette Hill. 610-828-7351. www.brittinghams.com.

Brownie's 23 East. 23 E. Lancaster Ave, Ardmore. 610-649-8389. www.brownies23east.com.

Chaps Taproom. 2509 W. Main St., Jeffersonville. 610-539-8722. www.chapstap.com.

THE DRAFTING ROOM. 900 N. Bethlehem Pike (Rt. 309), Spring House. 215-646-6116. www.draftingroom.com.

Drake Tavern. 304 Old York Rd., Jenkintown. 215-884-8900. www.draketavern.com.

Fatty's Bar and Grill. 812 E. Willow Grove Ave., Wyndmoor. 215-233-5909.

Finn McCool Tavern. 3120 Penn Ave., Hatfield. 215-721-0206.

Gullifty's. 1149 Lancaster Ave., Rosemont. 610-525-1851. www.gulliftys.com.

J.D. McGillicuddy's Pub. 2626 County Line Rd., Ardmore. 610-658-2626. www.jdmcgillicuddys.com.

Lucky Dog Saloon & Grille. 417 Germantown Pike, Lafayette Hill. 610-941-4652. www.theluckydogsaloon.com.

McKinley Tavern. 881 Township Line, Elkins Park. 215-576-9066.

McShea's Restaurant & Bar. 242 Haverford Ave., Narberth. 610-667-0510. www.mcsheas.com.

P.J. Whelihan's Pub. 799 Dekalb Pike, Blue Bell. 610-272-8919. www.pjspub.com.

Roache & O'Brien. 560 Lancaster Ave., Haverford. 610-527-6308.

The Shanachie Pub and Restaurant. 111 E. Butler Ave., Ambler. 215-283-4887. www.shanachiepub.com.

333 Belrose. 333 Belrose Ln., Radnor. 610-293-1000. www.333belrose.com.

Toad's Tavern. 8 East 1st Ave, Conshohocken. 610-828-1553.

UNION JACK'S PUB. 2750 Limekiln Pike, Glenside. 215-886-6014.

The Wild Onion. 900 Conestoga Rd., Rosemont. 610-527-4826. www.thewildonion.com.

DELAWARE

Catherine Rooney's Irish Pub. 1616 Delaware Ave. Trolley Sq., Wilmington. 302-654-9700. www.catherinerooneys.com.

KELLY'S LOGAN HOUSE. 1701 Delaware Ave., Wilmington. 302-655-6426. www.loganhouse.com.

NEW JERSEY

Chickie's & Pete's. 183 Rt. 130, Bordentown. 609-298-9182. www.chickiesandpetes.com.

Chickie's & Pete's. 6055 Blackhorse Pike, Egg Harbor Twp. 609-272-1930.

CORK. 90 Haddon Ave., Westmont. 856-833-9800.

FIREWATERS. Brighton and Boardwalk, Atlantic City. 609-344-6699.

Firkin Tavern. 1400 Parkway Ave., Ewing Township. 609-771-0100. www.firkintavern.com.

Harper's Pub. 1 Gibbsboro Rd., Clementon. 856-435-5655. www.harperspub.com.

HIGH ST. GRILLE. 64 High St., Mount Holly. 609-265-9199. www.highstreetgrill.net.

Jay's Elbow Room. 2806 Rt. 73 N., Maple Shade. 856-235-3687.

Mitchell's Café. $11^1/_2$ Church St., Lambertville. 609-397-9853.

P.J. Whelihan's Pub. 700 N. Haddon Ave., Haddonfield. 856-427-7888. www.pjspub.com.

P.J. Whelihan's Pub. 61 Stokes Rd., Medford Lakes. 609-714-7900. www.pjspub.com.

P.J. Whelihan's Pub. 425 Hurfville-Cross Keys Rd., Sewell. 856-582-7774. www.pjspub.com.

Plantation Restaurant & Bar. 7908 Long Beach Blvd., Harvey Cedars. 609-494-8191. www.plantationrestaurant.com.

W.L. Goodfellows. 310 E. White Horse Pike, Absecon. 609-652-1942. www.wlgoodfellows.com.

BEYOND

Arena Bar & Grill. 380 Coal St., Wilkes Barre. 570-970-8829. www.arenabarandgrill.com.

The Classic Rock-N-Roll Café. 233 W. Hamilton St., Allentown. 484-221-9945. www.classicrocknrollcafe.com.

THE FARMHOUSE. 1449 Chestnut St., Emmaus. 610-967-6225. www.thefarmhouse.com.

P.J. Whelihan's Pub. 4595 Broadway, Allentown. 610-395-2532. www.pjspub.com.

P.J. Whelihan's Pub. 1658 Hausman Rd., Allentown. 610-395-2532. www.pjspub.com.

CHAPTER 2

The Breweries

DOGFISH HEAD CRAFT BREWERY

Brewery: 6 Cannery Village Center, Milton, Del. 302-684-1000.

Brewpub: 320 Rehoboth Ave., Rehoboth Beach, Del. 302-226-2739.

Alehouse: 800 W. Diamond Ave., Gaithersburg, Md. 301-963-4847.

Web: www.dogfish.com

Head brewer: Brian Selders

Sam Calagione makes all those brews that "regular" beer drinkers like to make fun of.

His Dogfish Head brewery in Delaware makes beer with honey and chicory and pumpkin and grapes and apricots. These beers come with the kinds of goofy names—**Raison d' Etre** and **Au Courant**, for example—that Schwarzeneggers pounding Coors Light mock as "girly" beers.

Never mind that hairy-chested beer freaks around the world eagerly await each new flavor from Dogfish Head, that magazines from *Details* to *Money* have declared it as one of America's top three or four breweries, that it once made a beer that's as strong as schnapps. To many drinkers—the ones who never stray from their industrial American lagers—Calagione's beers aren't real American beers.

41

So, what are the boys on the corner going to say about **Liquor de Malt**?

Behind that funny French name is a bona fide high-octane malt liquor. In one of Calagione's typically zany marketing ploys, it's packaged in a 40-ounce, twist-off bottle wrapped in a brown paper bag.

OE800, move over.

INSIDE INFO

▶ It's named after a peninsula in Maine, where founder Sam Calagione's family had a summer cabin when he was a kid.

▶ When the brewery opened distribution in New Jersey, Calagione delivered the first case via boat, rowing himself across Delaware Bay from Lewes, Delaware, to Cape May, New Jersey.

▶ Randall the Enamel Animal is Dogfish Head's organoleptic hop transducer module. Or, in plain English, a three-foot-long cylinder packed with a half a pound of whole leaf hops affixed to a keg, through which tapped beer flows, further enriching it with hops flavors and aroma. Randall makes random appearances at area taverns.

- Calagione is author of *Brewing Up a Business: Adventures in Entre-preneurship from the Founder of Dogfish Head Craft Brewery* (Wiley, 2006), a high-spirited biography of his business ventures.
- The brewpub also distills rum, gin, and other spirits.
- The photogenic Calagione once modeled Levi Slates pants in a series of magazine ads.

6 ESSENTIALS

60-Minute IPA. A nicely balanced IPA brewed with a constant addition of hops during the one-hour boil. Inside sources say the "secret" hop is Simcoe.

Aprihop. Yes, it's made with apricots, but I'd give this the edge over Magic Hat No. 9.

Chicory Stout. A stout you can sip glass after glass, brewed with chicory, organic Mexican coffee, St. John's Wort, and licorice root.

Midas Touch Golden Elixir. A recipe based on DNA analysis from King Midas's tomb in Turkey, contains barley, white Muscat grapes, honey, and saffron.

Raison d'Etre. A brown ale made with beet sugar and raisins. Rich, complex, and a great value.

World Wide Stout. Once the world's strongest beer at about 25 percent alcohol, it is now reissued annually at a "mere" 18 percent. Surprisingly drinkable for something so strong.

OTHERS

90 Minute IPA, 120 Minute IPA, Indian Brown Ale, Lawnmower Light, Red & White wit, Black & Blue strong fruit ale, Burton Baton, Chateau Jiahu, Festina Peche, Punkin Ale, Snowblower Ale, Immort Ale, Olde School Barleywine, Raison d'Extra, Golden Era imperial pilsener, Pangea spiced ale, Fort strong fruit ale.

FLYING FISH BREWING CO.

Brewery: 1940 Olney Ave., Cherry Hill, N.J. 856-489-0061.

Web: www.flyingfish.com

Head brewer: Casey Hughes

New Jersey suds drinkers with a fondness for craft beer should say a prayer every night, thanking the heavens for Gene Muller and his Flying Fish Brewing Company Without his beer, the so-called Garden State—or at least the patch of strip malls south of Trenton—would be nothing but a vast Corona wasteland.

It is Flying Fish that—after years of sales efforts—finally broke into the bland, industrial tap mix at many of South Jersey's strip mall clubs, opening the door to other premium flavors. These days, when you find yourself elbowing the Coors crowd for a spot at the bar, at least you have a shot at coming up with a well-hopped pale ale.

I mean, geez, Flying Fish is even available in Applebees these days.

▶ The brewery produced a bottle-conditioned porter, but discontinued it in 2006. Sad, because it was one of the few locally made porters, a classic Philadelphia style. If you're lucky, you can still find bottles of its **Imperial Espresso Porter** released for the brewery's 10th anniversary in January 2007.

▶ Owner Gene Muller decided to open the brewery in the early '90s while driving home from the Great American Beer Festival (GABF) in Denver with his then-girlfriend and cofounder, Robin Tama.

▶ The brewers frequently release specialty hybrids of their standard ales. **Love Fish** is **Abbey Double** infused with cherries; **Puckerfish** is the same abbey that soured. **Black Fish** is **XPA + Porter**, and **Vanilla Ice** is iced **Grand Cru** flavored with vanilla beans.

▶ Because of high demand, Flying Fish Farmhouse beer is bottled at the F.X. Matt brewery in New York. Fish is hoping to build a new, larger facility in South Jersey.

▶ **HopFish IPA** was originally spelled "HopPhish"—until the brewery got a cease and desist letter from the Phish band's attorney. Ironically, during an earlier visit to Philly, the band's members toasted each other in the dressing room with bottles of FF.

▶ Sample many of the brewery's styles at the **Flying Fish Pub** at Campbell's Field, home of the Camden River Sharks.

6 ESSENTIALS

Belgian Abbey Double. Very malty with a fruity nose. A low-priced alternative to the real thing.

Belgian Grand Cru Golden Winter Ale. Strong, golden, and exceptionally warming at 7 percent alcohol. (October–February)

Extra Pale Ale. The brewery's best seller, XPA is the go-to brew on the upper deck at Citizens Bank Park.

Farmhouse Summer Ale. Light, very drinkable, lawnmower beer. Bring this to the softball game.

Hopfish IPA. Closer to an English version of India Pale Ale, more subtle and malt-based than those West Coast monsters.

Oktoberfish. An ale version of the classic German Oktoberfest, it's brewed with Dusseldorf alt yeast for a clean but spicy flavor. (September–November)

OTHERS

ESB Ale, Imperial Espresso Porter, Blackfish (half and half), **Big Fish Barleywine.**

RIVER HORSE BREWING CO.

Brewery: 80 Lambert Lane, Lambertville, N.J. 609-397-7776.

Web: www.riverhorse.com

Head brewer: Tim Bryan

This 12-year-old family-run outfit has always been known primarily for its **Special Ale** and **Hop Hazard**, basic hop treats that, while well regarded, don't exactly slap you upside the head. A couple years ago, though, the brewery gave itself a kick in the seat, redesigned its packaging, and bottled up a pair of Belgian-style ales.

Though both are high in alcohol, these two beers do not feel like huge head-bangers.

Jim Bryan, who founded River Horse with his brother Tim, explained, "A lot of times we brew to our own taste. We tend not to like some of the sweeter Belgian ales, so with the **Tripel**, especially, we were looking to go as high as we could with the alcohol without overpowering the taste of the beer." For anyone unfamiliar with the dynamic flavor of abbey-style Belgian beers, these ales are excellent primers.

You're not going to get rocked with a classic malt bomb like **Affligem Noel**. But drink two and you'll think you're in Antwerp's Kulminator tavern. Both are a nice step inside from the cold.

INSIDE INFO

▶ A river horse is a hippopotamus, which ancient Egyptians believed represented the beer goddess.

▶ The brewery operates out of the former O.T.C. oyster cracker bakery.

▶ Each year, hundreds of beer fans show up at the brewery's giant chili cook-off, part of the Lambertville–New Hope Winter Festival.

▶ Though there's no bar at the brewery, you can get ample tastes during tours that are run seven days a week.

▶ The two Belgians are available in a mixed case, called the Belgian Block.

▶ Unlike most area beers, RH can be tough to find on tap; the brewery's products are mainly bottled.

▶ In late 2007, the Bryans sold their company to investors in Philadelphia, who promise an expansion. The Bryans continue to work at the brewery.

SIX ESSENTIALS

Belgian Frostbite. Surprisingly well hopped for a Belgian-style dark ale. I wish this were available all year. (September–March)

Hop Hazard. This started out as an average pale ale, but it's growing on me.

Lager. Fairly run-of-the-mill lager, reminds me of Harp.

Special Ale. It's an ESB, the first brew out of the horse.

Summer Blond. Your basic easy-sipper. (April–August)

Tripel Horse. The absolute best from this brewery. Since it's 10 percent alcohol, buy a case of this Belgian-style tripel and don't worry about polishing it off immediately.

SLY FOX BREWERY & EATERY

Brewpub: Rt. 113, Pikeland Village Sq., Phoenixville, Pa. 610-935-4540.

Brewery and Brewpub: 312 N. Lewis Rd., Royersford, Pa. 610-948-8088.

Web: www.slyfoxbeer.com

Head brewer: Brian O'Reilly

Dressed in a T-shirt and tattered jeans—the usual, comfortable garb for a 30-something brewer—Brian O'Reilly seems at ease in the confined space of his brewhouse. Up and down a steel ladder, he busily adjusts valves and checks gauges.

"I've been doing this for years," he shrugs, paddling the porridge-like mash.

A native of New England, O'Reilly got his start by apprenticing in a couple of small New Hampshire breweries before taking a job with the John Harvard chain in Cleveland. He hit the local scene in '99 at New Road, the former Collegeville brewpub, where he quickly gained notice with a gold medal winner (a German-style pilsener) at the Great American Beer Festival.

After New Road's brewery went dry, O'Reilly spent a short spell at Victory in Downingtown before landing the Sly Fox gig in 2002. Within months, he showed that his first GABF medal was no fluke when America's most important beer-judging event handed O'Reilly a bronze for his **French Creek Helles**, a light lager.

Beer freaks noticed. You see a Sly Fox tap handle, you know you're going to get an expertly crafted brew with balanced flavor. Helles greets you like a routine thirst-quencher—the sort of thing you've been drinking since you turned 18. But it finishes with a remarkably rounded malt body that raises the stakes well above lawnmower standards.

It is pure and simple.

- ▶ Each spring the brewery hosts a goat race and names its annual bock after the winner.
- ▶ The brewpub, which started in Phoenixville, was the first local micro to can its beer, at its second brewery in Royersford.
- ▶ Sly Fox bottles New York's Southampton Ales for Philly-area distribution.
- ▶ It brews the annual anniversary wheat beer for the **Flanigan's Boathouse** restaurants in Conshohocken and Malvern.
- ▶ Each year, its IPA Project produces a series of India Pale Ales flavored with one specific hop variety. In December, it pours all of them at a one-day festival that also features **Odyssey**, an IPA with a blend of each hop.
- ▶ Its Incubus Belgian-style tripel is named after an evil spirit that has sexual intercourse with women as they sleep.

6 ESSENTIALS

Dunkel Lager. A dark, full-flavored Bavarian-style lager. (Fall, winter, canned)

O'Reilly's Stout. What I imagine Guinness tastes like when you're sipping in a Dublin pub.

Pikeland Pils. O'Reilly's signature beer, a bright medal-winner that holds its flavor in aluminum.

Royal Weisse. Yes, a wheat beer in a can. (Summer only)

Rt. 113 IPA. That "113" isn't just the name of the road, it's the IBU count, making this one of the bitterest beers in America.

Saison Vos. A light, spicy Belgian-style ale influenced by saison guru Phil Markowski of Southampton Brewing.

OTHERS

Black Raspberry Reserve, Ichor quadruppel, Instigator Doppelbock, Christmas Ale, Incubus tripel, Odyssey Imperial IPA, Oktoberfest.

STOUDT'S BREWING CO.

Brewery: 2800 N. Reading Rd. (Rt. 272), Adamstown, Pa. 717-484-4387.

Web: www.stoudtsbeer.com

Head brewer: John Matson

So you're on the wrong side of City Line and they won't let you back inside Philly. Where do you go now?

Head west on the Pennsylvania Turnpike, beyond the 'burbs to Adamstown, Lancaster County. This town would be a nightmare for anyone (i.e., adult male) who couldn't endure six or seven consecutive hours of shopping among rows and rows of dusty antiques. It would be if it weren't for Stoudt's Brewing Co.

The region's oldest microbrewer, Stoudt's runs a beer hall inside an antique mart and a well-stocked bar at its adjoining Black Angus restaurant. Almost everything they brew, including their wonderful **Triple**, is on tap.

I've always suspected the microbrewery was a slick business scheme by Ed and Carol Stoudt to lure reluctant men to their shopping bazaar. Under more sober circumstances, the typical male head of household might be somewhat circumspect about carefree spending on junk. But get the old man sauced on high-octane beer, and next thing you know, you're happily loading a pink flamingo into the car trunk.

I hate to admit this, friends, but Joe Six-pack is speaking from experience on this one.

INSIDE INFO

▶ Originally a German-style brewery, it now makes classic Belgian- and English-style ales as well.

▶ The brewery is run by Carol Stoudt, known as the First Lady of American Brewing because she was the nation's first female brewmaster.

▶ A number of area house beers are made by Stoudt's. **Willie Sutton Lager** at **Fairmount Grill** is **Fest**; **Leglifter Lager** at **White Dog Café** is **APA**.

▶ The brewery runs huge festivals throughout the summer and into October, with beers from dozens of East Coast breweries and a "best of the wurst" buffet.

▶ Stoudt's old 25-ounce bottles, which were phased out in '05, are making a comeback. **Fat Dog Imperial Oatmeal Stout** and **Old Abominable Barleywine**, both aged in whiskey barrels, are now in corked bombers.

6 ESSENTIALS

American Pale Ale. A good-drinking West Coast ale, perfectly suitable on draft.

Blonde Double MaiBock. Clean, golden, and smooth—try it with apple sausage.

Double IPA. Watch out! This beer is far stronger than it tastes. Beautiful balance, firmly hopped, excellent value. 10 percent alcohol.

Fat Dog Imperial Oatmeal Stout. Another deceptive head-banger at 9 percent. Black and roasty.

Gold Lager. One taste of this crisp German-style lager and you'll wonder why you ever drank Bud.

Triple. Once notoriously inconsistent, but now that it's in a 12-ounce bottle it's a tidy, little Belgian that's almost winelike in character.

OTHERS

Pils, Scarlet Lady ESB, Weizen, Oktoberfest, Winter Ale.

TROEGS BREWING CO.

Brewery: 800 Paxton St., Harrisburg, Pa. 717-232-1297.

Web: www.troegs.com

Head brewer: Chris Brugger

Christmas season '03 was the date that Troegs Brewing really caught my eye.

Before then, I'd been a fan of all of the brewery's well-made styles. But then it hit the streets with **The Mad Elf**, a spicy holiday ale. In the days after it was bottled, area beer distributors were besieged by a fevered run that cleared every single case off the shelves within 48 hours of delivery. Retailers reported numerous instances of customers ordering the beer weeks before delivery, and then showing up and filling their Toyotas with a half-dozen cases at a time.

A full month before Christmas, it was almost entirely gone.

"We figured we'd make enough to send two to five cases to each distributor; that would be enough," said Chris Trogner, who runs the brewery with his brother, John. "The plan was to put out enough bottles to sell from Thanksgiving to Christmas. "I don't even think we made it to Thanksgiving.

Today, the demand is just as strong, though—thanks to larger batches—it's a lot easier to put your hands on a case of **The Mad Elf**.

INSIDE INFO

▶ The brewery is run by brothers Chris and John Trogner; the brewery's name comes from a combination of *Trogs,* an old family nickname, and *kroeg,* a Flemish word meaning pub.

▶ Tours are Saturdays at 2 p.m. only, but the brewery sometimes opens its doors on other days for out-of-towners. Call ahead.

▶ An annual contest looks for the best artwork made with Troegs bottle caps.

▶ The anniversary house beers at the **Drafting Room** (Exton, Springhouse) are made by Troegs.

▶ Freshest Troegs outside the brewery: **McGrath's**, 202 Locust St., 717-232-9914, in downtown Harrisburg, with an excellent draft selection.

▶ Keep your eyes open for exceptionally rare, hand-corked, 3-liter jeroboams of **The Mad Elf**. Just don't Bogart it!

Dreamweaver Wheat. Right now, this is the best wheat beer made in America, period.

HopBack Amber. The flagship label, named for the chamber used to add extra hops before fermentation. Very aromatic and well balanced.

The Mad Elf. A holiday beer made with honey, cherries, and chocolate malt. A spectacular Belgian-style ale, with complex layers of flavor. 11 percent. (November–January)

Nugget Nectar. An amped-up version of HopBack, they call it an "imperial amber ale" with intense hop (Tomahawk) flavors. (February)

Sunshine Pils. Bright and crisp with the added bonus of a Saaz hops bath. Find this on draft. (May-August)

Troegenator Double Bock. One of *Playboy* magazine's top beers in America. Rich, malty, well balanced.

OTHERS

Pale Ale, Oatmeal Stout. Rugged Trail brown ale.

VICTORY BREWING CO.

Brewery: 420 Acorn Lane, Downingtown, Pa. 610-873-0881.

Web: www.victorybeer.com

Head brewer: Ron Barchet

Anton Dreher's cold, stiff hand has a hold on Bill Covaleski's mortal soul.

Dreher, one of the 19th century's great European brewers, has been dead and buried for 140 years. Covaleski, the 40-something co-founder of Downingtown's Victory Brewing, is a highly regarded member of America's new generation of craft brewers.

At first sip, it's hard to see the connection.

Dreher is widely regarded as the father of modern lager; it was his recipe for Vienna lager that provided the DNA for the Spaten brewery's first Oktoberfest beer in 1841. Yet the cynic could easily blame Dreher—and his European ideals of purity—for ultimately leading the brewing industry toward a strict adherence to established styles. Lager, at its worst, is all about conformity.

Covaleski, by contrast, is best known as an ale man. Like most microbrewers, he rejected many of the stale conventions of insipid, factory-made lager. As a fan of his bitter, aromatic **HopDevil Ale**, I found it impossible to conceive of Covaleski's paying his respects to Dreher.

And yet, a few years ago when we stood in a snowstorm at Dreher's mausoleum on the outskirts of Vienna, I could see Covaleski welcome the Austrian's frosty grip. "I guess this is where it all began," Covaleski said, giving in to Dreher's pull.

INSIDE INFO

▶ Co-owners Covaleski and Ron Barchet have been friends since they met on a school bus when they were kids.

▶ The brewery is housed in the former Pepperidge Farm bakery in Downingtown.

▶ One of its most collectible bottles is **Ten Years Alt**, the first doppel-sticke alt—an unusual Dusseldorf-style ale—to be produced in America.

▶ In addition to 12-ouncers, the brewery also produces corked 750ml bottles of **V-Twelve** strong ale and **V-Saison**, suitable for cellaring.

▶ Each Christmas it bottles **Hop Wallop**, an excessively hopped ale that quickly sells out at area distributors.

▶ **Victory HopDevil** is on tap at **Rex's** in West Chester, but it's hard to find. It's poured from a tap handle labeled, in honor of Homer Simpson, "Duff Beer."

6 ESSENTIALS

Golden Monkey. This delicious Belgian-style golden ale is one of the best values in Philly beer because it packs so much punch and flavor at about the same price as an average imported lager.

HopDevil. The flagship brand is an assertive India Pale Ale fermented with yeast that was used in the classic, old Ballantine Pale Ale recipe.

Old Horizontal. Rich, dark, warming—the beer to feed your friends stuck on Bigfoot Ale.

Prima Pils. A German-style pilsener with a crisp hops finish. It was named the grand champion pilsener for four straight years in the United States Beer Tasting Championship.

Storm King Imperial Stout. A rich, high-alcohol stout that—despite the strength—you can suck down all night. The best imperial stout in America, period.

Victory Lager. A light, crisp Helles—the beer to feed your friends stuck on Bud Light.

St. Boisterous Maibock, Sunrise Weissbier, Throwback Lager, Whirlwind Wit, Festbier, Hop Wallop imperial IPA, Moonglow Weizenbock, St. Victorious doppelbock, V-Twelve Belgian strong ale, V-Saison.

WEYERBACHER BREWING CO.

Brewery: 905 Line St., Easton, Pa. 610-559-5561.

Web: www.weyerbacher.com

Head brewer: Dan Weirback

After all these years, I still haven't made up my mind about beer aged in bourbon casks.

Part of me says man was meant to drink whiskey from a shot glass, followed by a suitable chaser. The other part of me says, I'm too lazy to wash the damn glasses; let's do boilermakers.

Heresy is Weyerbacher's incredibly smooth **Old Heathen** imperial stout steeped in a used oak bourbon barrel. If you've had this within six inches of your nose, you wouldn't need me to tell you

that—the sweet bourbon aroma wafts off the black brew like Sunoco's finest on a summer afternoon in Marcus Hook.

A couple of glasses in a hot room have me sweating in overdrive; maybe it's the 8 percent alcohol content. But before collapsing, I detect vanilla, chocolate, and a bit of fruitiness (figs?).

I'm going to pack a few bottles away till the temperature drops and I dry off. In the meantime, the flavor should mellow.

INSIDE INFO

- ▶ In addition to **Heresy**, Weyerbacher ages two others in wood: **Insanity** (**Blithering Idiot**) and **Prophecy** (**Merry Monks**).
- ▶ The brewery is named after founder Dan Weirback, who was a home brewer.
- ▶ Tours: Saturday afternoons, with free samples. Bring a Weyerbacher growler for draft-to-go or mix your own variety cases.
- ▶ Look for the Big Beer variety case, an excellent deal that contains **Merry Monks**, **Blithering Idiot**, **Old Heathen**, and **Raspberry Imperial Stout**.

6 ESSENTIALS

Blanche. If you like **Hoegaarden**, give this locally made version of a Belgian white ale a try.

Blithering Idiot. The best-named barleywine in the world. A monster beer (11 percent alcohol) with layers of flavor.

Double Simcoe IPA. That bright, fresh aroma is from the new Simcoe hops, a specialty variety that's the darling of craft brewers nationwide.

Hops Infusion. A new recipe pumps up the flavor in this IPA.

Merry Monks. Nice yeast character from this Belgian-style tripel.

Old Heathen Imperial Stout. This style was originally brewed in England for the Russian czars. With seven types of malt, this roasty brew could help you survive a Siberian winter.

OTHERS

Autumn Fest, Black Hole dark ale, Heresy, Imperial Pumpkin Ale, Insanity, Old Heathen, Prophesy, Quad, Raspberry Imperial Stout.

YARDS BREWING CO.

Brewery: 901 N. Delaware Ave. Philadelphia. 215-634-2600.

Web: www.yardsbrewing.com

Head brewer: Josh Ervine

They're brewing beer again in Kensington.

More than 40 years after the crusty neighborhood's last brewery went belly-up, a small crew of devoted beermakers has returned to boil hops and bottle suds. You can smell the malt from Frankford Avenue, just below Lehigh, where the towering brick smokestack marks the site of the old Weisbrod & Hess Oriental Brewery.

It's now the home of Yards Brewing.

In a relocation that took nearly a year, the brewery moved its equipment eight miles east and rehabbed Weisbrod & Hess's long-idled bottling plant.

Yards made its first "official" delivery with a horse-drawn beer wagon, with brewery founder Tom Kehoe at the reins. "Not a bad ride," said Kehoe as he jumped off and grabbed a pin (a mini keg) of his Yards ESA.

He might have been talking about the history of his growing brewery.

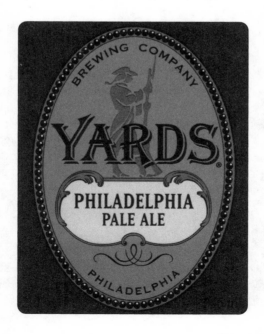

INSIDE INFO

▶ The brewery, founded by two college pals, started out in a small Manayunk garage, once used as a bread bakery.

▶ Some of its beers are fermented in open tanks, an old English brewing technique in which a pillow of yeasty foam atop the ale protects it from contamination.

▶ **Ales of the Revolution** is a series of Yards beers based on early Philadelphia recipes in partnership with the **City Tavern**. In addition to **Poor Richard's Tavern Spruce** (below), the brewery bottles the strong, golden **Thomas Jefferson Ale** and **General Washington Tavern Porter**.

▶ In 2007, Kehoe split with his former partners, who will continue to brew at the Kensington facility under the name of Philadelphia Brewing (see p. 66). Kehoe plans to open a new and larger brewhouse in early '08 at Poplar Street and Delaware Avenue in Northern Liberties.

6 ESSENTIALS

Extra Special Ale. The first real post-Prohibition ale bottled in Philadelphia. Known simply as ESA, it's best when poured from a cask by a hand pump.
India Pale Ale. Kensington's answer to that famous Downingtown IPA. This ale isn't as devilish, but it's an excellent quaff just the same.
Love Stout. No longer brewed with oysters to add body, but it's still a smooth-drinking dark ale.
Philadelphia Pale Ale. It took years for the brewery to perfect this recipe. Now, thanks to Simcoe hops, it's the city's standard pale ale.
Poor Richard's Tavern Spruce. Based on Ben Franklin's 18th-century recipe, it's made with an actual spruce tree in the boiling kettle.
Saison. A very refreshing summertime Belgian ale, with hints of spice.

OTHERS

Thomas Jefferson Ale, George Washington Tavern Porter, Trubbel de Yards abbey-style double, Pynk raspberry ale, Chateau Kenso Belgian-style ale.

D.G. YUENGLING & SON, INC.

Brewery: 5th and Mahantongo streets, Pottsville, Pa.
570-622-4141.

Web: www.yuengling.com

Brewmaster: Mike Brennan

Not that it matters around here, but there are about a thousand different lagers in the world.

There's pilsener, of course. And bock and Oktoberfest and dunkel and helles and Dortmunder. Budweiser's a lager, and so are Coors, Miller, Genesee, Stroh's, Rolling Rock, PBR, and Schmidt's. Same with most popular imports—Heineken, Labatt's, Beck's, Harp, Corona, Tecate, Dos Equis are all lagers. And so are some of the more obscure labels, like Aass and Czechvar and smoky Schlenkerta Rauchbier.

Basically, any beer made with yeast that ferments at a relatively cool temperature at the bottom (not the top) of the vat is a lager. Most everything else is an ale.

Hell, even light beer is lager.

There are a thousand different lagers out there. But in the city that practically invented the American version of this popular beer, lager means only one thing: **Yuengling Traditional Lager**. Belly up to almost any bar in Philadelphia and say "lager," and the bartender'll pour you Yuengling.

INSIDE INFO

▶ Once and for all, it's pronounced YING-ling.
▶ Founded in 1829, it's the oldest brewery in America. Canada's Molson (est. 1786) is the oldest brewery in North America.
▶ During Prohibition, Yuengling made ice cream. Its dairy continued to operate into the 1980s.
▶ Some fans call it "Vitamin Y."
▶ Though it's sold only on the East Coast, it is now the fifth largest brewer in America.
▶ In addition to its plants in Pottsville, Yuengling bottles in the former Stroh's plant in Tampa, Florida.

6 ESSENTIALS

Light Lager. The *only* light beer in this book. This one actually has some decent flavor and body. (I still won't drink it!)

Lord Chesterfield Ale. A huge hop surprise that was once fairly common on draft in the city. Alas, it's mainly available only in mixed cases these days.

Original Black & Tan. The only locally made black and tan, it's a mildly roasty mix of **Premium** and **Porter**.

Porter. Not a true porter because it is bottom-fermented. Who cares? For much of the '70s, this (along with **Prior Double Dark**) were the only dark beers available in Philly. Still a very good value.

Premium. Almost impossible to find, it's a pilsener that is lighter and a bit sweeter than **Lager**.

Traditional Lager. I know many who won't drink anything else. Why? The flavor is decent enough, but this is a matter of pride. It's a homegrown alternative to BudMillerCoors.

OTHER BREWERIES

APPALACHIAN BREWING CO.

Brewery: 50 N. Cameron St., Harrisburg, Pa. 717-221-1080.
Web: www.abcbrew.com
Head brewer: Artie Tafoya

Inside info: In addition to its full-scale brewery/restaurant in Harrisburg, Appalachian runs brewpubs in Gettysburg and Camp Hill.

Essentials:
Purist Pale Ale, Jolly Scot Scottish Ale, Mountain Lager, Water Gap Wheat, Hoppy Trails India Pale Ale, Susquehanna Stout, Peregrine Pilsner, Kipona Fest.

BARLEY CREEK BREWING CO.

Brewery: Sullivan Trail and Camelback Rd., Tannersville, Pa. 570-629-9399.
Web: www.barleycreek.com
Head brewer: Tim Phillips

Inside info: Poconos brewpub distributes some kegs in the Philly area and several styles in 12-ounce bottles.

Essentials:
Antler Brown Ale, Rescue IPA, Navigator Golden Ale, Angler Black Lager.

DOCK STREET BREWERY

Brewery: 701 S. 50th St., Philadelphia. 215-726-2337.
Web: www.dockstreetbeer.com

Inside info: The city's newest brewpub is also a long-time "contract" brewery, producing beer in kegs and bottles out of the F.X. Matt plant in Utica, N.Y.

Essentials:
Illuminator bock beer, Amber.

LANCASTER BREWING CO.

Brewery: 302 Plum St., Lancaster, Pa. 717-391-6258.
Web: www.lancasterbrewing.com
Head brewer: Christian Heim

Inside info: Temporarily closed a couple years ago, it's now back and operating at full steam, with longtime area brewer Bill Moore at the kettles.

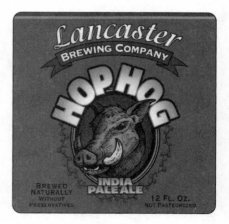

Essentials:
Franklinfest, Milk Stout, Strawberry Wheat, Hop Hog, Amish Four Grain Ale, Gold Star Pilsner.

LEGACY BREWING CO.

Brewery: 545 Canal St., Reading, Pa. 610-376-9996.
Web: www.legacybrewing.com
Head brewer: Scott Baver

Inside info: Up–and–coming brewery is pushing the envelope with several of its styles (and labels).

Essentials:
Midnight Wit, Hedonism Ale; and **Euphoria, Bixler's Alt, Triple H** (all draft only).

LION BREWERY

Brewery: 700 N. Pennsylvania Blvd., Wilkes-Barre, Pa. 570-823-8801.
Web: www.lionbrewery.com
Head Brewer: Bob Klinetob

Inside info: Contract brewer produces low-priced Pocono and Stegmaier labels.

Essentials:
Pocono Lager, Pocono Caramel Porter, Stegmaier Porter, Lionshead. Look also for limited seasonals, including **Brewhouse Bock**.

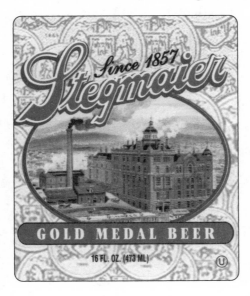

PHILADELPHIA BREWING CO.

Brewery: 2439 Amber St., Philadelphia. 215-427-2739.
Web: www.philadelphiabrewing.com

Inside info: Upon the 2007 breakup of Yards Brewing, partners Bill and Nancy Barton founded the city's newest brewery at the site of the former Yards brewery.

Essentials: No new brands were disclosed as of press time.

TWIN LAKES BREWING CO.

Brewery: 4210 Kennett Pike, Greenville, Del. 302-658-1826.
Web: www.twinlakesbrewingcompany.com

Inside info: Newest brewery in the vicinity, it's located on a family farm five miles outside of Wilmington. Tours on Wednesday and Saturday afternoons.

Essentials:
Route 52 Pilsner, Greenville Pale Ale, Tweeds Tavern Stout (on tap only).

MY FAVORITE BEERS

CASEY PARKER ▸ co-owner, Jose Pistola's

1. Rodenbach Grand Cru. First time I had it was this year, and without a doubt it's my favorite beer in the world.

2. Petrus Oak Aged Pale Ale

3. Orval

4. Delirium Nocturnum

5. Nodding Head Ich Bin Ein Berliner Weisse

6. Boon Kriekenlambic

CHAPTER **3**

The Brewpubs

I'll take Philadelphia's cozy neighborhood taverns over those boring
suburban P.J. McStripmall Eateries any day. But when it comes to
brewpubs, I've gotta admit, the 'burbs have the city beat, hands
down.

There are all of four brewpubs inside the nation's sixth biggest
city.

Cross City Avenue and head mostly west, and you're welcomed
not by the scent of cow pastures but by the sweet aroma of freshly
cooked malt and simmering hops.

In the nearby suburbs, there are no fewer than 20 brewpubs.

And more are coming.

PHILADELPHIA

DOCK STREET BREWERY

701 S. 50th St.   215-726-2337
Web: www.dockstreetbeer.com
Head brewer: Scott Morrison

Rosemarie Certo, one of the partners in the original (and now closed)
Dock Street brewpub on Logan Square, returned to the beer scene in
2007 with a smaller, comfier place in the Cedar Park section of West

Philly. Located in a former firehouse, it hopes to be an anchor for this edgy neighborhood's growth.

MANAYUNK BREWERY & RESTAURANT

4120 Main St.   215-482-8220
Web: www.manayunkbrewery.com
Head brewer: Chris Firey

Nothing to blow your socks off. But what do you want? This place caters to Main Street's pickup crowd. **Schuylkill Punch** says it's a Belgian red, but it's raspberry Kool-Aid. If you're lucky, the hefe or the bock is on tap—grab a glass and sit out on the deck.

ABOUT BREWPUBS

Brewpubs are taverns where beer is brewed on the premises. Often you'll see the large stainless steel or copper tanks behind glass doors.

Typically, they offer a range of basic flavors, including a light ale or lager, a pale ale, a wheat beer, a hoppy ale (ESB or IPA) and a dark beer (porter or stout). Your best bet is to order a flight, usually a two-ounce serving of each beer on tap, then settle in on a favorite.

Be sure to try one of the nonregular taps – better brewpubs offer one or more seasonals or specialties, such as a Belgian-style ale or cask-conditioned ale. These often show off the brewer's talents the best.

Enjoy the beer? Order a growler to go. This is a half-gallon (4 pints) of fresh beer drawn from the tap. A growler usually costs about $12, depending on the style, with refills running as little as $8. Some brewpubs allow you to refill a growler from any brewpub, others insist on using their own.

Word to the clueless: Don't ask for a Bud or some other factory beer. It's like ordering a Big Mac in a family restaurant. Here's your chance to try something different; enjoy the craftsmanship of the brewmaster.

NODDING HEAD BREWERY & RESTAURANT

1516 Sansom St.   215-569-9525
Web: www.noddinghead.com
Head brewer: Gordon Grubb

The city's best brewpub, no contest. **Ich Bin Ein Berliner Weisse** is a world-class German-style sour wheat ale, **Grog** is a filling brown ale. Other notables: **Monkey Knife Fight** (ginger), **George's Fault** (coriander and honey) and **3C Extreme** (imperial IPA). Forget about parking; stop by the excellent cigar shop downstairs.

TRIUMPH BREWING OLD CITY

117-121 Chestnut St., Old City   215.625.0855
Web: www.triumphbrew.com
Head brewer: Patrick Jones

Opened in spring '07. Smaller than Triumph's other two locations, but the beer is about the same. Food served on small pallets. Should be an outstanding addition to Old City's already active beer scene, especially with Jones—a big winner at the '05 GABF—at the helm.

THE 'BURBS

IRON HILL

Iron Hill is a locally owned chain that continues to expand. Its newest location is Lancaster, and there have been persistent rumors that it is looking at Center City and South Jersey.

Overall, though, this is a chain that doesn't feel like a chain.

Yes, all Iron Hill brewpubs feature the same basic menu of affordable fare and these beers: **Light Lager, Raspberry Wheat, Lodestone Lager, Anvil Ale, Ironbound Ale, Pig Iron Porter**. All are well made and even (in the case of the porter) outstanding. But beer freaks know to pass by those and go straight for seasonal beers, including summertime wheat beer and cold-weather barleywine, and other specials, including full-bodied, high-alcohol Belgian beasts.

Even when you don't see anything interesting on the tap list, ask to see the list of aged 750ml bottles (available to go). These are excellent specialties, including sour Flemish-style ale, barrel-aged blends and Iron Hill's ass-kicking **Russian Imperial Stout**. They're expensive (up to $20) but worth the price, and you can cellar them for years.

Once a month, the locations take turns hosting a Brewer's Reserve, which features a single beer from each pub, often matched with ales from outside breweries.

If I have one gripe, it's this: Iron Hill seems to attract an inordinate number of families with kids, so either hang out late at night or expect grubby, little monsters to annoy the hell out of you.

CRABBY LARRY'S BREW PUB

237 W. Butler Ave., Chalfont   215-822-8788
Web: www.crabbylarrys.com
Head brewer: John Stecker

The area's most lightly regarded brewpub has never seemed to hit its stride. But Stecker, who hails from a nearby homebrew supply shop, seems to be getting some of the beers (eight different taps!) into shape. I'm optimistic about its future. Mainly seafood on the menu.

PORTERHOUSE RESTAURANT & BREW PUB

5775 Lower York Rd., Lahaska   215-794-9373
Web: www.porterhousepub.com
Head brewer: Dean Brown

A tidy brewpub where you can wash off the dust after a day at Rice's Market. The house ales are vastly improved now that Brown, a familiar face in the Philly brewing scene, is on board.

TRIUMPH BREWING NEW HOPE

400 Union Square Dr., New Hope   215-862-8300
Web: www.triumphbrew.com
Head brewer: Brendan Anderson

Smart, clean, and surprisingly comfy for a shopping center tavern. The beer varies from the pedestrian to the superb. Best bet: whatever's on the hand pump.

AIMEE PROZAN ▶ bartender, Nodding Head

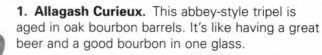

1. Allagash Curieux. This abbey-style tripel is aged in oak bourbon barrels. It's like having a great beer and a good bourbon in one glass.

2. Nodding Head Ich Bin Ein Berliner Weisse. This sour/tart wheat beer is low in alcohol. It is a great beer for summer. Refreshing and thirst-quenching, it's a perfect beer to drink during a shift (not that I drink during my shift).

3. Yards Pynk. This is a Belgian-style raspberry wheat and is pretty new. I love the flavor and the color of this beer. Excellent for tailgating.

4. La Fin du Monde. This 9 percent alcohol Belgian-style tripel (there's a trend here) is from Canada. I think it's one of the best values; you can usually pick up a case for around $45.

5. Westvleteren 12. One of the best beers ever. Stellar.

6. Dogfish Head Chateau Jiahu. Were there any beer styles 9,000 years ago? This beer is light and malty, with floral overtones. Also, the best label Sam Calagione has put on any of his products.

CHESTER COUNTY

IRON HILL PHOENIXVILLE

130 E. Bridge St., Phoenixville   610-983-9333
Web: www.ironhillbrewery.com
Head brewer: Tim Stumpf

Because it's the smallest of Iron Hill's locations, this could well evolve into the most creative. Small batches mean the brewer will be more willing to experiment with exotic styles. Meanwhile, the **Lodestone Lager** (Munich-style) here is the best version I've had. Outdoor seating is planned, and the menu is well priced; try pairing the crab-stuffed shiitake mushrooms with **Anvil Ale**.

IRON HILL WEST CHESTER

3 W. Gay St., West Chester   610-738-9600
Web: www.ironhillbrewery.com
Head brewer: Chris LaPierre

Located in a former Woolworth's store, this one has the warmest feel in the chain. Nice patio, an ideal spot to enjoy Sunday brunch (11 a.m.–2 p.m.). Look for LaPierre's Belgian-style brews, including a massive quadruppel and a barleywine.

MCKENZIE BREW HOUSE MALVERN

240 Lancaster Ave., Malvern   610-296-2222
Web: www.mckenziebrewhouse.com
Head brewer: Ryan Michaels

This mammoth brewpub with an outdoor deck and huge downstairs game room with pool tables is an oasis along the western Main Line. Fairly basic range; ask for the specialties or ask for large bottles to go.

SLY FOX BREWERY & RESTAURANT PHOENIXVILLE

519 Kimberton Rd., Phoenixville   610-935-4540
Web: www.slyfoxbeer.com
Head brewer: Brian O'Reilly

The suburbs' most innovative brewpub continues to turn out a huge assortment of flavors. O'Reilly's annual IPA Project features a monthly ale made with a single hop variety; the year's selections are served together at an annual early-December fest. In the spring, a goat race is an excuse to drink lots of bocks.

VICTORY BREWING

420 Acorn Ln., Downingtown   610-873-0881
Web: www.victorybeer.com
Head brewer: Ron Barchet

Most Victory fans are familiar only with the brewery's fine bottled products, but the brewpub is a can't-miss destination. In addition to all the regulars served fresh (**Golden Monkey** is never better than here), you'll find one-time-only specials, including single-hop pilsener and harvest ale. Enjoy decent food, including excellent pizza, in a cavernous beer hall; make sure you stop for Victory souvenirs and beer-to-go in the spacious gift shop.

DELAWARE COUNTY

IRON HILL MEDIA

30 E. State St., Media   610-627-9000
Web: www.ironhillbrewery.com
Head brewer: Bob Barrar

Generally considered Iron Hill's best brewer, big Bob is known for barrel aging and a *huge* Russian imperial stout.

MCKENZIE BREW HOUSE GLEN MILLS

451 Wilmington Pike, Glen Mills   610-361-9800
Web: www.mckenziebrewhouse.com
Head brewer: Ryan Michaels

Your basic variety of light-gold-pale-amber-brown-oatmeal is for the nonadventuresome. You'll have to search for Michaels's better brews, including award-winning Scottish wee heavy. In the meantime, head downstairs and check out the foosball, darts, shuffleboard, billiards, and 60" flat-screen in the Underground Pub.

LEHIGH COUNTY

ALLENTOWN BREW WORKS

812 Hamilton St., Allentown   610-433-7777
Web: www.thebrewworks.com
Head brewer: Beau Baden

Just opened in the summer of 2007, it's the son of Bethlehem Brew Works. Features an outdoors Biergarten and a classy downstairs lounge.

BETHLEHEM BREW WORKS

569 Main St., Bethlehem   610-882-1300
Web: www.thebrewworks.com
Head brewer: Beau Baden

A modern joint in the middle of Bethlehem's redeveloped district. Decent food and an uneven variety of taps. Avoid the stuff that's light enough for your kid sister and proceed directly to very commendable lambics. Firkins on the first Thursday of each month; Belgians downstairs at the Steelgaarden lounge. Look also for bottles (via Weyerbacher) of **Pumpkin Ale** and **Rude Elf's Revenge**.

MONTGOMERY COUNTY

G.G. BREWERS

282 Keswick Rd., Glenside   215-887-0809
Head brewer: Gerry A. Martin III

Smallest brewpub in the vicinity, across the street from the Keswick Theater. Beer quality ranges from OK to, um, OK. Taste everything, because Martin doesn't exactly hew to any style standards. (A 13 percent weizenbock?!)

GENERAL LAFAYETTE INN & BREWERY

646 Germantown Pike, Lafayette Hill   610-941-0600
Web: www.generallafayetteinn.com
Head brewer: Chris Leonard

An underrated gem with widely varying styles. **Chocolate Thunder Porter, Alt! Who Goes There?** and **Cuvee de Lafayette** are all strongly flavored. Grab **Pacific Pale Ale** if you see it on cask. Avoid the blue-hair dining room and hang in the bar, where the atmosphere is lively and the menu is the same. Large bottles of aged ale available for consumption inside the bar; ask for the cellar list.

IRON HILL NORTH WALES

1460 Bethlehem Pike, North Wales   267-708-2000
Web: www.ironhillbrewery.com
Head brewer: Larry Horwitz

Fairly spartan pub, but this is the one Iron Hill where you're most likely to find an offbeat ale, thanks to the always inventive Horwitz. (When he worked at Manayunk Brewing, he made "stone" beer, a completely obscure process involving steaming rocks.) Huge bar, great spot to catch a game on the flat-screens. Join the mug club for deals and early word on special brews.

ROCK BOTTOM

160 N. Gulph Rd., King of Prussia   610-230-2739
Web: www.rockbottom.com
Head brewer: Brian McConnell

Located in a corner of KofP mall, this is the Macy's of American brew-pubs, with a few stylish but hard-to-find bargains in the midst of a bunch of boring Dockers. The **Schwarzbier** won silver at the GABF in '06, but I've never seen it on tap; the imp stout is quite good. Horrible service and the food is dull.

SLY FOX BREWERY & RESTAURANT ROYERSFORD

312 Lewis Rd., Royersford   610-948-8088
Web: www.slyfoxbeer.com
Head brewer: Brian O'Reilly

Somewhat larger than Sly Fox's original joint in P-ville, this one offers the same outstanding variety of brews. I'm less than overwhelmed by the kitchen, though. Wander to the back to catch a glimpse of the brewery's canning operation.

DELAWARE

DOGFISH HEAD BREWING & EATS

320 Rehoboth Ave., Rehoboth Beach   302-226-2739
Web: www.dogfish.com
Head brewer: Michael Gerhart

A bit of a shore bar dive, though very comfy, with excellent entertainment. But you're here for Dogfish's beers, and you won't find them any fresher—or more fascinating—than here. Look especially for one-offs that are not part of DFH's usual bottles. And don't forget to try one of the homemade flavored spirits. Chocolate vodka!

IRON HILL NEWARK

147 E. Main St., Newark   302-266-9000
Web: www.ironhillbrewery.com
Head brewer: Justin Sproul

The original Iron Hill is as good as ever, tucked along a lively street just off the campus of U. of D. In the summertime, make sure you get a glass of hefeweizen.

IRON HILL WILMINGTON

710 S. Madison St.,Wilmington   302-658-8200
Web: www.ironhillbrewery.com
Head brewer: Brian Finn

Handsome restaurant on a massive parking lot along Wilmington's scenic Riverwalk. Avoid Kahunaville and head directly for a pint of Finn's **Anvil Ale**. Nice upstairs deck, hang out after a Blue Rocks game.

STEWART'S BREWING

219 Governor's Sq., Bear   302-836-2739
Web: www.stewartsbrewingcompany.com
Head brewer: Ric Hoffman

Another shopping center brewpub, but don't let that fool you. Hoffman's turning out a solid range on his tiny system, including a full-flavored pilsener and an outstanding smoked porter.

NEW JERSEY

TRIUMPH PRINCETON

138 Nassau St., Princeton   609-924-7855
Web: www.triumphbrew.com
Head brewer: Tom Stevenson

Nice downtown Princeton feel to this joint, and the beer selection is always a surprise. Smokey rauchbier is a favorite, and give the **Roggenbock** a try—it's flavored with caraway seeds.

TUN TAVERN

200 Kirkman Blvd, Atlantic City   609-347-7800
Web: www.tuntavern.com
Head brewer: Tim Kelly

The second-best place to drink draft beer in A.C. (after **Firewaters**), which isn't completely faint praise. Most of the spigots have little distinct character, but it's all very drinkable and if you're lucky there's a special with some spunk. Free parking (with validation) in the lot directly across the street.

CHAPTER **4**

The Beer

STYLES

One of the things I hate to hear, usually from women, is, "I hate beer."

I tell them if you think you don't like beer, it's because you haven't found the beer you like. Usually they sniff and tell me they've already tasted 'em all, then they go back to their Chablis.

Look, there are hundreds of different types of beer with vast differences in color, aroma, body, alcohol, and, most importantly, flavor. Beer can be sweet or sour, light or dark, bitter or malty, thirst-quenching or a perfect complement to dinner. A person who says all beer is the same is either a dunce or a wine industry operative.

This guidebook offers just a sampling of the wealth of varieties on the market today.

Beer is generally divided into two categories, based on its fermentation.

Ales are fermented at warmer temperatures for short periods with yeast that works from the top. This method tends to impart more distinct flavors that may be either fruity or spicy.

Lagers are fermented at cooler temperatures for longer periods with yeast that works at the bottom. Lagers tend to have a crisp, clean taste.

Within these two categories, there are dozens of styles and substyles. The main varieties are below. For more detail, I urge you to find a copy of *Michael Jackson's Beer Companion* (Running Press, 2000).

When you find a beer you like, remember two things: its brewery and its style. Chances are, you'll find something else you like from the same brewery or within the same style.

Get out there and explore. One of the reasons Philly is the Best Beer–Drinking City in America is that you can find exceptional examples of nearly every variety of beer, brewed right here in our town.

ALE

Altbier. A German brown ale, conditioned (or aged) like a lager, it's exceptionally drinkable with a very good malt and hops balance. Example: **General Lafayette Alt! Who Goes There?**

Barleywine. Not a wine, but a very strong dark beer with an intense, fruit-like malt and hop balance. Example: **Dogfish Head Olde School Barleywine**.

Belgian-style double. Rich, somewhat sweet with fruit-like aroma, very little bitterness. Example: **Flying Fish Belgian-style Dubbel**.

Belgian-style golden. Complex, somewhat sweet and quite strong, similar to Belgian tripel. Example: **Victory Golden Monkey**.

Brown ale. Roasty, nutty, and dark, with a light body. Example. **Troegs Rugged Trail**.

Double IPA. Pumped-up India Pale Ale, with more malt and an extreme hop presence and higher alcohol. Example: **Dogfish Head 90 Minute IPA**.

Extra Special Bitter (ESB). Medium hops bitterness with a noticeable malt presence, well balanced and very drinkable. Example: **River Horse Special Ale**.

Fruit. Can be sweetened, but its better versions tend to be tart, a result of fermentation with wild yeast. Example: **Dogfish Head Aprihop**.

Hefe-weizen. A classic German unfiltered, frothy wheat beer with a huge fruit or spice aroma and refreshing flavor. Example: **Stoudt's Weizen**.

Imperial stout. Huge, powerfully malty body with burnt, roasted flavor, high alcohol, ink-black color. Example. **Victory Storm King**.

India pale ale (IPA). Pale golden, with intense, herbal hop aroma and high bitterness. Example: **Victory HopDevil**.

Kolsch. An ale version of a pilsener with mild hops and light body. Example: **General Lafayette Germantown Blonde**.

Pale ale. Pale, crisp-tasting, often with grapefruit-like fruitiness. Example: **Yards Philly Pale Ale**.

Porter. Dark with a balanced bitterness, frequently flavored with smoke or fruit. Example: **George Washington's Tavern Porter** (Yards).

Scottish ale. Copper colored, sweet, and rich; full body with low hops and some smokiness. Example: **Appalachian Jolly Scot**.

Stout. Can be dry (Irish stout) or sweet (cream stout); American versions tend to be almost chocolatey. Example: **O'Reilly's Stout (Sly Fox)**.

Weizenbock. A dark wheat beer with a spicy aroma and high alcohol. Example: **Victory Moonglow**.

White. A cloudy, easy drinking brew with citrus aroma, a result of the yeast, which is often unfiltered. Example: **Weyerbacher Blanche**.

Wild ale. Beer that is intentionally infected with a "wild" yeast (Brettanomyces, aka "Brett"), creating a funky aroma and tart flavor. Example: **Dogfish Head Festina Peche**.

LAGER

American amber lager. Somewhat maltier than light lager, with nonexistent hops. Example: **Yuengling Lager**.

American pale lager. Pale, fizzy, and yellow, with a mild malt presence. Example: **Stegmaier 1857**.

Bock. Strong malt flavor with very light bitterness, somewhat warming. Example: **Lancaster Spring Bock**.

WHADDYA WANT?

Looking for	Go local
Basic Pennsylvania lager	Yuengling
The cheapest	Lionshead
The rarest	Victory Baltic Thunder
Other than Sierra Nevada Pale Ale	Yards Philly Pale
Drink all night	Stoudt's Gold
Really bitter	Sly Fox Rt. 113 IPA
Really sweet	Flying Fish Belgian Style Dubbel
Really tart	Nodding Head Ich Bin Ein Berliner Weisse
Highest alcohol	Dogfish Head World Wide Stout (18%)
A big bottle to bring to a party	Iron Hill vintage Old Ale 750 ml
A softball game	A sixpack of canned Sly Fox Phoenix Pale Ale
A barbeque	Victory Fest
A celebration	Victory St. Victorious
Completely off the wall	Midas Touch Golden Elixir
Wean your pal off Bud Lite	Iron Hill Light Lager
Chick beer	Yards Pynk
Better than Hoegaarden	Weyerbacher Blanche
Better than Guinness	Sly Fox O'Reilly's Stout
Tailgater beer	Flying Fish Extra Pale Ale
Something decent on Main St., Manayunk	Manayunk Brewing I'll Be Bock
Double bock	Stoudt's Smooth Hoperator
Wheat beer	Troegs Dreamweaver Wheat
Tart fruit	Sly Fox Black Raspberry Reserve
Sweet fruit	Lancaster Strawberry Wheat
A fight	Nodding Head Monkey Knife Fight
To get laid	Bethlehem Elongator Doppelbock
After you strike out	Yards Love Stout

Go nuts

Straub

Make your own

Westvleteren 12

Meantime India Pale Ale

Three Floyds Pride & Joy

Russian River Pliny the Younger

Gouden Carolus D'Or

Panil Barriquee

Samuel Adams Utopias (25%)

Troegs Mad Elf jeroboam

A keg of Brooklyn Lager

Aecht Schlenkerla Helles

Bosteels Deus Brut Des Flanders

Liefmans Gluhkriek (warmed to 110°)

Weihenstaphaner Original

Lindemans Framboise

Hitachino Next White Ale

North Coast Old No. 38

10 cases of Flying Fish Extra Pale Ale

Stone Oaked Aged Arrogant Bastard at Flat Rock Saloon

Weltenburger Kloster Asam-Bock

Schneider Weisse

Cantillon Rose de Gambrinus

Redbach

Orkney Skull Splitter

Legacy Euphoria

Thirsty Dog Old Leghumper

Dortmunder. Clean, golden, and crisp, with light bitterness and dry finish; quite refreshing. Example: **Iron Hill Lodestone Lager.**

Double bock (doppelbock). Big, strong, and malty, with a roasty edge and high alcohol. Example: **Troegs Troegenator.**

Dunkel. Rich and smooth, exceptionally drinkable, and, despite its color, quite refreshing. Example: **Penn Dark**.

Helles. The German answer to pilsener (it means *bright*), it is somewhat maltier, with lighter hops. Example: **Stoudt's Gold Lager**.

Imperial pilsener. A new variety that's light in body but high in alcohol, with a strong hops character. Example: **Dogfish Head Golden Era.**

Maibock. A lighter version of bock with plenty of sweet, bready malt. Example: **Stoudt's Blonde Double Mai Bock**.

Marzen/Oktoberfest. Copper-colored, full-bodied, and toasty, a perfect accompaniment to many foods. Example: **Victory Festbier.**

Pilsener. Bright, crisp, and clear, with a floral aroma and floral hops; very refreshing. Example. **Lancaster Gold Star Pilsner.**

Vienna. Rich, toasted malt flavor, light hops and light body. Example: **Triumph Vienna Lager.**

GERMAN BEER

I manage to miss Oktoberfest nearly every year because, despite the impeccable precision of the Germans, the Munich beer-drinking event is actually held in September.

Why, I'm not sure. Maybe they use a different calendar.

Maybe I'm being picky, but I tend to assume that a festival named after a certain month should, in real life, be held in that very month. In this case, that would be *October*.

And why not? The mouth-warming, malty amber lagers brewed for Oktoberfest are perfect autumn refreshers. You want to drink them when the leaves are falling, during an Eagles game, maybe, with sausages and kraut and an oompah band.

Some years, though, the local temperatures are still in the 90s when Oktoberfest rolls around.

I speak from experience; you just can't play the tuba when you're sweating into your lederhosen.

DRINK HERE

Hearty fare and the Reinheitsgebot:

The Austrian Village. 321 Huntingdon Pike, Rockledge. 215–663–9902. Excellent, cheap food (Wiener Schnitzel for $8.50) and **Dinkel Acker** on tap.

Blue Ox Bistro. 7980 Oxford Ave., Fox Chase. 215-728-9440. www.blueoxbistro.com. It's lost a bit of its old world charm (and German menu) since reopening in '06, but you'll still find a glass of **Spaten Optimator**.

The Cannstatter Bar & Restaurant. 9130 Academy Rd., Northeast Philly. 215-332-0121. www.cvvphilly.com. This German social club hosts regular festivals with folk dancers, oom-pah music, and **Warsteiner**. Its restaurant is open to the public with an amazingly cheap $6.50 platter on Thursday nights.

Ludwig's Garten. 1315 Sansom St., Center City. 215-985-1525. www.ludwigsgarten.com. Two bars with a raft of tap handles that don't waste any space on losers. Look especially for **Schneider Aventinus** and **Ayinger Celebrator**, two bocks you rarely see on draft. Pair 'em with a heaping plate of spaetzle.

Newportville Inn. 4120 Lower Rd., Newportville. 215-785-6090. www.newportvilleinn.net. This "American tavern with a German accent" gives you a fine taste of Munich's best (**Lowenbrau, Spaten, Hacker-Pschorr**), perfect for washing down the Schweine Braten.

Otto's Brauhaus. 233 Easton Rd., Horsham. 215-675-1864. Biggest German tap selection in the 'burbs, with 23 spigots, including **Franziskaner, Hofbrau, Ayinger.** Excellent breakfast (Hansel and Gretel pancakes with apple strudel and ice cream!), even if you're not hoisting a stein.

DRINK THIS

Guaranteed: better than Beck's:

Doppelbock. A bit more strength and body than a standard bock, known as "liquid bread." Look for beers that end in *-ator*, a nod to the original, **Paulaner Salvator**. Classic: **Ayinger Celebrator**.

Dunkel. A dark lager that's not as ponderous as it looks. Surprisingly refreshing, especially in the late summer. Classic: **Ettaler Kloster**.

Hefeweizen. It's unfiltered wheat ale with the yeast still in the glass. Full of banana and clove aroma—a great breakfast beer. Classic: **Franziskaner**.

Kolsch. Cologne's answer to Czech pilsener, it's a light, delicately hopped ale with a fruit-like aroma. Classic: **Gaffel**.

Marzen/Oktoberfest. Copper-colored lager with a sweet malt finish, created to honor Munich's huge annual fest. Classic: **Hacker Pschorr**.

Weizenbock. Not a true bock, because it's an ale. Here, the bock means extra flavor, extra strength. Classic: **Schneider Aventinus**.

DRINK THIS, TOO

Immigrants left their mark on local beer:

Appalachian Mountain Lager. A Dortmunder-style lager from Harrisburg.

Flying Fish Octoberfish. A top-fermented ale version of the autumn lager.

Penn Dark. OK, it's from Pittsburgh, but (a) owner Tom Pastorius is a Philly guy, and (b) this is a superb Munich dunkel.

Sly Fox Instigator. There's that *-ator*, and this doppelbock— available in large bottles—measures up to the best.

Stoudt's Weizen. I'm not a fan of American-made hefeweizen, but here's one worth loading in the fridge in July.

Victory Festbier. Full bodied with a hint of smoke in the aroma.

" How much beer is in German intelligence? "

—Friedrich Nietzsche

BRUSSELS, USA

I had dinner once with beer expert Michael Jackson at Monk's Café, and he marveled upon draining a glass of draft Achel, an obscure Trappist monastery ale. "This beer," he exclaimed, "has never been seen anywhere outside of Belgium. It's never even been consumed outside the brewery."

Pardon me for the shrug, but we're kinda used to this sort of thing around here.

Philadelphia was the first American city to regularly serve Belgian ale on tap. It was the first to serve **Rodenbach**, draft **Chimay**, **Cantillon**, and **Kwak**. We guzzle so much gueuze, wit, lambic, saison, and other Flemish specialties that nearly every local micro now feels obliged to compete with its own version of Belgian ale.

And most of those measure up quite nicely against the originals.

DRINK HERE

6 joints that specialize in Belgian beer:

Abbaye. 635 N. 3rd St., Northern Liberties. 215-627-6711. Excellent neighborhood feel, decent chalkboard menu.

Bridgid's. 726 N. 24th St., Fairmount. 215-232-3232. www.bridgids.com. A welcoming horseshoe bar inspires great conversation over **Chimay Blue.**

Eulogy Belgian Tavern. 136 Chestnut St., Old City. 215-413-1918.
www.eulogybar.com. Funkier than Monk's, huge bottle selection.

Monk's Café. 264 S. 16th St., Center City. 215-545-7005.
www.monkscafe.com. Has conquered more Belgians than
Napoleon. Phenomenal tap list.

Steelgaarden. 569 Main St., Bethlehem. 610-882-1300.
www.thebrewworks.com. Hard to pull yourself away from the
craft beers of Bethlehem Brew Works upstairs.

Zot. 122 Lombard St., Headhouse Square. 215-639-3260.
www.zotrestaurant.com. A quiet haunt away from the South
Street scene.

DRINK THIS

6 outstanding Belgians available in Philly:

Affligem Dubbel. Often overlooked but possibly the classic double.

Bavik Wittekerke. Put down that Hoegaarden; this is a better white
beer.

Gueuze Vigneronne Cantillon. Tart, funky, wine-like (but don't
hold that against it).

Rochefort 10. Made by Trappist monks, dark and sublime.

St. Bernardus Abt 12. As close to Westvleteren 12 as you can get
without flying to Belgium.

Urthel Samaranth. Sweet and spicy quadruple.

DRINK THIS, TOO

6 locally made "Belgians":

Flying Fish Belgian Abbey Double. Outstanding value.
Legacy Midnight Wit. Very spicy with nice fruit undertones.
Stoudt's Triple. Nose-tingling aromatics, potent head-banger.
Victory Golden Monkey. As close to Duvel as you can get in
America.
Weyerbacher Merry Monks' Ale. Huge reams of flavor.
Yards Saison. Nicely spiced, very drinkable in August.

IRISH BARS

What happened to the leprechauns?

Used to be, the begorra buggers were dancing their happy jig on
every other barroom wall, splashing mugs of green beer amid mead-
ows of marshmallow shamrocks. The height-deprived imps were the
official symbol of the blessed holiday.

These days, though, when you stop in for a quick one at any of
the 20 or so Irish pubs between the rivers in Center City, you'll find
hardly a one of the lucky charmers.

It's as if they never existed!

In fact, leprechauns are a dirty word inside the city's new "authentic" breed of Irish pubs. At woodsy, handcrafted bars where the staff
speaks with a brogue, the dancing demons have been summarily ban-
ished with the brutal efficiency of a high school disciplinarian.

DRINK HERE

There are too many Irish pubs in Philly to count. Here's a cross-section:

AUTHENTIC®

Downey's Restaurant. 526 S. Front St. South Street area.
215-625-9500. www.downeysrestaurant.com. This old-time
classic is actually the city's first pre-fab pub; its furnishings are
from a former Irish bank.
Fado. 15th and Locust streets, Center City west. 215-893-9700.
www.fadoirishpub.com. Shepherd's pie meets the Stepford
Wives.

The Plough & the Stars. 123 Chestnut St., Old City. 215-733-0300. www.ploughstars.com. Excellent food, but a nightmare on weekends.

Tir na Nog Irish Bar & Grill. 1600 Arch St., City Hall area. 215-514-1700. www.tirnanogphilly.com. Very good menu in a very convenient location. Stop in before grabbing a train from Suburban Station.

MY FAVORITE BEERS

JODI McCORMACK ▸ bartender, Monk's Cafe

 1. Guinness Stout. The brew I grew up with. As a poor student in Dublin I would give blood on a Monday because they would fill you with Guinness afterwards until you felt better. We would wander over from Trinity to the Hopstore and suffer through the tour so we could enjoy a couple of free pints at the end. The best pint I've ever had was on a very rainy night in O'Cathain's in Ballyferriter outside Dingle. I wasn't even expecting it. You've never been in a more unassuming pub. My mouth is watering right now thinking about the creaminess of that pint.

2. Chimay Grand Reserve. And so I came to America and, in 1991, the Guinness here was atrocious. I was not a lager drinker so there was really nothing for me. Somebody introduced me to the White Russian and I put on two stone (28 pounds) that summer. I then found myself in Philadelphia where the Guinness was no better, so I turned to Mr. Jameson, until one day a bartender who knew of my plight took me to the Copa and told me they had just the thing for me, and that was the day I met Chimay Grand Reserve. At last there was a beer I could drink in America. And that was the beginning of me and the Belgium Beers.

3. Gouden Carolus Grand Cru of the Emperor

4. t'Smisje Calva Reserve

5. Malheur Brut

6. Cantillon Rose de Gambrinus

IS THAT FLANN O'BRIEN AT THE END OF THE BAR?

The Bards. 2013 Walnut St., Center City west. 215-569-9585.
www.bardsirishbar.com. You know that friend of yours from
St. Joe's who just returned from a two-week sabbatical in County
Cork with a fake brogue? I think I saw him bingeing on
Bushmill's at the end of the bar.

The Black Sheep. 247 S. 17th St., Rittenhouse Square. 215-545-9473.
www.theblacksheeppub.com. A neighborhood gem.

Fergie's Pub. 1214 Sansom St., Center City east. 215-928-8118.
www.fergies.com. Young, serious crowd that thinks it's in Dublin.

McGillin's Old Ale House. 1310 Drury St., Center City east.
215-735-5562. www.mcgillins.com. Sample T-shirt: Irish today,
hung over tomorrow.

WHERE IT'S ST. PADDY'S DAY EVERY DAY

Finnigans Wake. 537 N. 3rd St., Northern Liberties. 215-574-9240.
www.finnigans.com. Billed as the largest Irish pub and
entertainment complex in the East, it's a noisy, fun, four-level
hall populated by huge, noisy beer-drinkers. A gift shop carries
Irish stuff for your home.

Irish Pub. 2007 Walnut St., Rittenhouse Square, 215-568-5603; 1123 Walnut St., Center City east. 215-925-3311. www.irishpubphilly.com. Traditional wooden bar, small rooms, very casual.

McGlinchey's Bar & Grill. 259 S. 15th St., City Hall area. 215-735-1259. The lucky leprechaun lives. And so does green beer.

O'Neal's. 611 S. 3rd St., South Street area. 215-574-9495. www.onealspub.com. Best beer selection in an Irish pub, served by anti-Guinness separatists.

THE 'BURBS

Brittingham's Irish Pub. 640 Germantown Pike, Lafayette Hill. 610-828-7351. www.brittinghams.com.

Burke's Inn. 25 E. Eagle Road, Havertown. 610-449-4323.

Callahan's Tavern. 7403 West Chester Pike, Upper Darby. 610-352-9608.

Gillane's Tavern. 43 Cricket Ave., Ardmore. 610-896-1622.

Maggie O'Neill's. 1062 Pontiac Road (Pilgrim Gardens Shopping Center), Drexel Hill. 610-449-9889. www.maggieoneills.com.

McCloskey's Restaurant. 17 Cricket Ave., Ardmore. 610-642-9280.

McFadden's Tavern. 7319 West Chester Pike, Upper Darby. 610-352-9724.

Paddy Rooney's Pub. 449 West Chester Pike, Havertown. 610-446-9882. www.paddyrooneyspub.com.

Roache & O'Brien. 560 Lancaster Ave., Haverford. 610-527-6308.

The Shanachie Pub and Restaurant. 111 E. Butler Ave., Ambler. 215-283-4887. www.shanachiepub.com.

Sligo Pub. 113 W. State Road, Media. 610-566-5707.

Sumney Tavern. 1610 West Point Pike, Lansdale. 215-699-5693. www.thesumneytavern.com.

KILDARE'S PUB

This hugely successful local chain draws a young crowd to five (and counting) area locations (www.kildarespub.com):

- ▶ 4417 Main St., Manayunk. 215-482-7242.
- ▶ 509 S. 2nd St., Head House Square. 215-574-2995.
- ▶ 828 Dekalb Pike, King of Prussia. 610-337-4772.
- ▶ 1145 W. Baltimore Pike, Media. 610-565-8886.
- ▶ 18 W. Gay St., West Chester. 610-431-0770.

> ❝ Drink is the curse of the land. It makes you
> fight with your neighbor. It makes you shoot at
> your landlord and it makes you miss him. ❞
>
> —Irish proverb

DRINK THIS

*For a nation with an unmatched beer-drinking heritage, you wonder
why it doesn't produce more variety.*

Beamish. The official beer of the great Guinness boycott.
Very creamy.

Guinness. So much lore surrounds this stout; too bad the flavor
got sucked out a decade ago.

Harp. C'mon, Dick Yuengling kegs that stuff without breaking a
sweat at half the price.

Murphy's. Not as good as Guinness, but it'll do in a pinch.

O'Hara's. A newbie whose stout is already winning awards.

Smithwick's. I can only imagine it tastes better in Ireland because
the draft they pour here is about as remarkable as week-old
Wonder Bread.

DRINK THIS, TOO

6 American takes on Irish beer:

Bare Knuckle Stout. Do not be deceived; this is an Anheuser-Busch
Guinness clone. Still, it's passable.

Donnybrook Stout. Victory's dry stout is full flavored, with an
exceptionally smooth body (draft only).

Hooker Irish Red. The Connecticut brewery started sending Philly
its beer in '06. It's what you'd call a "session" beer—drink it all
night.

Kell's Irish Style Lager. Look for this award-winning lager in
22-ounce bombers, from Oregon's Rogue Ales.

Killian's Red. Avoid this Coors product at all costs. Just plain awful.

O'Reilly's Stout. This dry stout from Sly Fox (named after the
brewer) has more flavor than Guinness, and it's been showing up
on taps outside the brewpub (draft only).

IRISH PUBS WITHOUT GUINNESS?

A small group of Philly tavern owners have banned Guinness since 2000 over allegations of the multinational conglomerate's apparent commercial involvement with the Fado chain of Irish pubs. They refuse to pour Guinness, charging that its sale helps finance the slick tavern chain.

Most have replaced Guinness with the perfectly suitable Beamish Stout. Others pour O'Reilly Stout instead.

ERIN EXPRESS

A weekend or two before St. Paddy's Day, a group of Irish pubs sponsors an afternoon of free bus transportation around town. The buses are free and shuttle drinkers every half hour. If you drink fast, you can grab a Guinness in no fewer than a dozen different joints.

For info, look for posters in Irish pubs starting in February or visit the Express's infrequently updated web site, www.phillytown.com/erinexpress.htm.

A second Erin Express runs through the Northeast, and a similar Shamrock Shuttle runs down Frankford Avenue.

An unnecessary warning: Although it's a fun party, these annual events typically dissolve into a drunken mess.

BLACK & TAN

Order one in a Philly Irish pub and you'll likely get Guinness and Harp, unless you ask for Bass. Yuengling makes a beer called Black & Tan—essentially a mix of its Porter and Premium—so you may get that instead. Sly Fox makes an excellent black and tan, with O'Reilly Stout atop Phoenix Pale Ale.

❝ Here's to a long life and a merry one.
A quick death and an easy one. A pretty girl and an honest one. A cold beer and another one! **❞**

—Irish toast

FOR REAL IRISH

The Ancient Order of Hibernians runs several clubs around town where draft beer flows like the River Shannon. At the city's largest, the historic Division 39 (7229 Tulip St., Tacony), $10 will get you all the beer and sandwiches you want during Eagles, Notre Dame, or Penn State football games, from whistle to whistle. Membership for men 16 years and older who are practicing Roman Catholics of Irish birth or descent. www.aoh39phila.com.

TO THE EXTREMES

Now that the new millennium is well underway, we've got ourselves a new beer style.

No, we're not talking low-carb beer.

It's imperial India pale ale and, yes, that is a mouthful.

Take a look around at local micros and brewpubs, and nearly every one of them is producing an Imp, also known as a Double IPA. The style takes its name from Imperial Stout, a super-strong black beer that got its name from the English brews made for Russian czars.

There's no royalty involved in this bitter ale. In the case of India Pale Ale, the new imperial style means more of everything. It's maltier, more bitter, and it smells like your back yard just after you finished mowing the lawn.

DRINK THIS

6 Philly imperial IPAs (no descriptions—just breathe in the garden-like aroma and savor):

Bethlehem Brew Works Imperial IPA (draft only).
Dogfish Head 90 Minute IPA.
Nodding Head 3C Extreme Ale (draft only).
Stoudt's Double IPA.
Victory Hop Wallop.
Weyerbacher Double Simcoe IPA.

DRINK THIS, TOO

6 other over-the-top Philly beers:

Dogfish Head 120 Minute IPA. Takes that 90 Minute IPA to the next, bitter step.

Dogfish Head WorldWide Stout. At up to 25 percent alcohol, there's a sixpack in every bottle.

Flying Fish Vanilla Ice. It's FF's Grand Cru, iced to raise the alcohol to 14 percent, then flavored with vanilla beans. A rarity (draft only).

Stewart's Smoked Porter. Two-time GABF medallist is flavored with smoked malt. On tap at the brewpub each September (draft only).

Troegs Mad Elf. Flavored with cherries and honey, but it's the yeast that adds the spice (available at Christmas).

Weyerbacher Insanity. Blithering Idiot barleywine aged it in oak bourbon casks.

PHILLY FACT

Sam Calagione, the envelope-pushing brewer at Delaware's Dogfish Head Brewery, wrote the book on extreme beer. Literally. It's *Extreme Brewing* (Quarry Books, 2006), a recipe book for homebrewers looking to copy some of his outlandish ales.

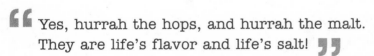

“ Yes, hurrah the hops, and hurrah the malt. They are life's flavor and life's salt! ”

—From the opera *Martha*,
Wilhelm Friedrich Riese, 1847

REAL ALE

The happy keg tends to froth about, emitting disgusting effluent. But what you get is a living, breathing animal of a brew. This secondary fermentation conditions the beer, producing natural carbon dioxide.

The taste difference is obvious even to novices. The artificial carbonation in mass-produced beer tends to feel crisper in the mouth. Think of an ice-cold 12-ounce can of Bud. Real ale is softer, but—contrary to popular myth—it is not flat. At its best, it nails your senses with a powerful, flowery hop aroma, tempered with a rich malt flavor. Think of a fresh-baked, seeded loaf of Amoroso's.

This is real ale—50 degrees and no artificial CO_2. The best way to taste malt, hops, and yeast, pulled by bartenders with beefy arms.

DRINK HERE

6 joints with real ale on old-fashioned hand-pumps:

700. 700 N. 2nd St., Northern Liberties. 215-413-3181.

Abbaye. 637 N. 3rd St., Northern Liberties. 215-627-6711.

Dawson Street Pub. 100 Dawson St., Manayunk. 215-482-5677. www.dawsonstreetpub.com. Three hand-pumps, one always pouring **Yards ESA**.

Fergie's Pub. 1214 Sansom St., Center City. 215-928-8118. www.fergies.com.

O'Neal's. 611 S. 3rd St., South Street area. 215–574–9495. www.onealspub.com.

Standard Tap. 901 N. 2nd St., Northern Liberties. 215-238-0630. www.standardtap.com.

Most brewpubs also serve at least one of their beers on a so-called beer engine.

DRINK HERE, TOO

6 joints with real ale outside the city:

The Drafting Room. 635 N. Pottstown Pike, Exton, 610-363-0521; 900 N. Bethlehem Pike, Spring House, 215-646-6116. www.draftingroom.com.

The Farmhouse. 1449 Chestnut St. Emmaus. 610-967-6225. www.thefarmhouse.com.

Flying Pig Saloon. 121 E. King St., Malvern. 610-578-9208.

Half Moon Restaurant & Saloon. 108 W. State St., Kennett Square. www.halfmoonrestaurant.com. 610-444-7232.

Spinnerstown Hotel Restaurant. 2195 Spinnerstown Rd., Spinnerstown. 215-536-7242. www.spinnerstownhotel.com.

Ugly Oyster Drafthaus. 21 S. 5th St., Reading. 610-373-6791. www.theuglyoyster.com.

DRINK THIS

6 cask-conditioned draft ales:

Flying Fish Extra Pale Ale. A good ballpark brew (available at the Citz) is an even better rugby ale on cask.

Fraoch Heather Ale. Never one of my favorites out of a bottle, but on cask it's a gem.

Lancaster Milk Stout. Double the smoothness.

Orkney Skullsplitter. A Scottish-made Wee Heavy that comes off like a Belgian barleywine.

Victory HopDevil. Those big hops balance even better with the malt.

Yards ESA. The classic Philly cask ale.

Though perfectly fine served from more common CO_2 bar taps, these ales improve when the kegs are properly conditioned and served on hand pumps..

FIRKIN AROUND

For an even "purer" cask-conditioned ale, try one served from a gravity-fed keg; that is, one without a pump.

Beer bars occasionally hoist one of these "firkins" (a small keg) onto a bar, pound a faucet into the bung and let the beer spill into your glass—give it a try. At Bethlehem Brew Works, they do it the first Thursday of the month, with proceeds donated to a local charity.

Or, head to the Northeast for the Grey Lodge Pub's Friday the Firkinteenth festival on, yes, every Friday the 13th. In just a few hours of elbow bending, you can sample the finest beers made in the region, served at traditional cellar temps to bring out their best flavor. It's loud, it's fun, and I guarantee the spilled beer will wash out of your Levis.

Bethlehem Brew Works. 569 Main St., Bethlehem. 610-882-1300.

The Grey Lodge Pub. 6235 Frankford Ave., Mayfair. 215-624-2969.

> **❝** Coach: 'Can I draw you a beer, Norm?'
> Norm: 'No, I know what they look like.
> Just pour me one.' **❞**

—Cheers

DOWN WITH BEER

Even quirkier: the Down Draft at Bridgid's. The tap hangs from the ceiling over the bar, where it drains beer from a keg sitting in an upstairs room. The contraption, invented by former Philadelphia beer entrepreneur Jim Anderson, pours pure cask ale.

Bridgid's. 726 N. 24th St., Fairmount. 215-232-3232. www.bridgids.com.

SECRET KEGS

Buried in the deepest corner of your favorite beer bar lies a stash of one of the world's greatest brews.

It's been guarded jealously, hidden from sight, untouched by meddlesome bartenders. Even regular customers who know the tap list by heart have never caught a whiff.

This fine beer—probably an ale, but maybe a hearty lager—was aged for years, maybe even a decade. It's a flavor so rare that those who are lucky enough to swallow a drop will talk about it for years.

And only the lucky ever get a taste.

What is this fine brew?

It's the Secret Keg—a perfectly preserved barrel that the owner's been holding, waiting for the perfect occasion to finally tap it open.

DRINK HERE

Ask for something from the cellar:

Flying Pig Saloon. 121 E. King St., Malvern. 610-578-9208. The owner is building up a nice list of old ale—ask for the cellar list. Try **Stille Nacht**, the Christmas beer from Belgium.

Gen. Lafayette Inn & Brewery. 646 E. Germantown Pike, Lafayette Hill. 610-941-0600. www.generallafayetteinn.com. Ask to see the bottle menu, and don't even think twice about ordering **The Phantom**, an aged barleywine.

Iron Hill Brewery. Locations in Media, North Wales, Lancaster, Phoenixville, and West Chester, Pennsylvania; and Wilmington and Newark, Delaware. www.ironhillbrewery.com. The brewpub chain is releasing large bottles of its specialties to go. Some, like the **Russian Imperial Stout**, are mellowing nicely after a year.

Monk's Café. 264 S. 16th St., Center City west. 215-545-7005. www.monkscafe.com. You've gotta be a reg'lar, but from time to time the owners will pull something special out of the cooler downstairs. And, keep your eye open for aged kegs that sometimes appear on the beer list.

Tria Café. 123 S. 18th St., Center City west. 215-972-8742. www.triacafe.com. Serves vintage bottles of **J.W. Lees Harvest Ale**, an English barleywine.

Way back in the corner of your local distributor. Unfortunately, some distributors aren't exactly meticulous when it comes to rotating their stock. If it's a dusty case of stout, go for it. If it's Ortlieb's circa 1968, you might want to pass.

DRINK THIS

If you have a cool, dark space, you can do it yourself.

Chimay Grand Reserve. Maybe the best candidate for cellaring; I tasted a 30-year-old bottle that was still effervescent and beautifully mellowed.

Gouden Carolus D'Or. Actually, I wouldn't drink this beer till it was aged at least a year. It's way too blunt in the first months.

Lindemans Cuvee Rene. Next time you buy a bottle of this Belgian gueuze, buy a second and stow it. It'll be perfectly drinkable for 10 years.

Samichlaus. Now that Austria's Castle Eggenberger is brewing this Christmas lager, the recipe changes slightly each year. Save and compare them through the years.

Sierra Nevada Big Foot Ale. In addition to its evolution into a complex, balanced beer, this barleywine has the added benefit of a dated bottle cap, making it easier to keep track of the years.

Victory Storm King. Whenever I buy a case of this excellent imperial stout, I can never finish it off. So I just shove a sixpack to the back of my cellar and scarf it down a year later.

MY FAVORITE BEERS

Former Phillies announcer **ANDY MUSSER** now a representative of Anchor Brewing, names his favorite beer joints around the country.

1. The Ginger Man. 11 E. 36th St., New York City. 212-532-3740. www.gingermanpub.com. 67 taps, and they're *all* fresh.

2. RFD. 810 7th St. NW, Washington, D.C. 202-289-2030. www.rfdwashington.com. More draft beer than its co-managed and more famous elder, The Brickskeller.

3. Capital Ale House. 623 E. Main St., Richmond, Va. 804-643-2537. www.capitalalehouse.com. With an ice strip down the back of the bar, you can keep your beer as cold as you'd like.

4. Falling Rock Tap House. 1919 Blake St., Denver, Co. 303-293-8338. www.fallingrocktaphouse.com. A huge selection—and just two blocks from Coors Field.

5. Standard Tap. 901 N. 2nd St., Northern Liberties. 215-238-0630. www.standardtap.com. Only beers brewed within 75 miles or so; nice gimmick, but they miss some great beers as a result.

6. Maggiano's. The Plaza at King of Prussia Mall. 610-992-3333. www.maggianos.com. OK, it's not a beer bar, but they have two taps devoted to **Anchor,** and I love their food!

HINTS FOR AGING GRACEFULLY

Beer should be relatively high in alcohol (over 8 percent). Barleywine and imperial stout are good candidates.

Some highly hopped beer can be aged, too. Try an Imperial IPA, but don't go much past a year because the hops tend to break down after that.

Try to keep your beer cool (not cold), at least in the mid 60s. The most important thing is to maintain a consistent temperature.

Keep it out of the light. Sunshine and incandescent light skunks your beer.

Stand the bottle upright, even if it's corked.

Crack open a bottle from time to time to chart progress.

> **❝** A fine beer may be judged with only one sip,
> but it's better to be thoroughly sure. **❞**

—Bohemian proverb

BEER FOR WINOS

Champagne? More like *sham*-pagne, if you ask me.

Every New Year's Eve, it's the same ol' swill: overpriced bottles of sweet, fizzy, bad wine posing as a drinkable beverage worthy of celebration.

An entire year goes by, and none but the most pretentious puckered-palates touch the stuff.

But flip the calendar and, pop, we're shooting corks and slopping the bubbly like Fred Astaire and Ginger Rogers in *Top Hat*.

Champagne is rich people's booze, priced to pinch your wallet hard enough to make you think you're buying something special.

Dom Perignon at 160 bucks a bottle? The grapes are no different from regular wine, and it's no harder to make, so howcum it's so expensive?

DRINK THIS

6 wine-like beers, for those stuck on grapes:

Dogfish Head Midas Touch Golden Elixir. Made with barley, white Muscat grapes, honey, and saffron. **Compare it to:** Sauterne.

Framboise Boon. A raspberry lambic from Belgium whose wild yeast produces a sparkle in the glass. **Compare it to:** Rosé.

Gueuze Vigneronne Cantillon. Tart, dry, with a touch of grape from the muscats added during maturation. **Compare it to:** Muscat d'Alsace.

Ich Bin Ein Berliner Weisse. The world-class tart wheat ale from Nodding Head Brewery & Restaurant. **Compare it to:** Sauvignon Blanc.

Miller High Life. The Champagne of beers! **Compare it to:** Chateau Luzerne American Chablis.

Weyerbacher Blithering Idiot. It's barleywine from the lush vineyards of the Lehigh Valley. **Compare it to:** Port.

6 wine bars with good beer, when you're stuck with those still stuck on grapes:

Amada. 217 Chestnut St., Old City. 215–625–2450. www.amadarestaurant.com. The Spanish wine bar's house IPA is **Sly Fox**. **O'Reilly's Stout, Yards Saison, Prima Pils** also on tap. And don't miss the fine tapas menu, including slices of Cerdo Iberico, the delicate deli ham from those cute, acorn-fed, black-footed pigs.

Ansill. 627 S. 3rd St., South Street area. 215-627-2485. www.ansilfoodandwine.com. You can expect a drinks list designed by wine pro Marnie Old to include some unusual brews, and this one doesn't fail. Check out **Unibroue's Ephermere-Apple** from Canada on tap.

Bar Ferdinand. 1030 N. 2nd St., Northern Liberties. 215-923-1313. www.barferdinand.com. You might be tempted by the inexpensive ($2 happy hour) Spanish house wine glasses, but the beer list has plenty of surprises, including impossible-to-find **Alhambra Negro**.

Cork. 90 Haddon Ave., Westmont, N.J. 856-833-9800. When your friend drags you to one of those stiff-collared wine dinners, you'll perk up when you get a look at that offbeat (**Maudite, Fullers ESB**) tap list.

Tria. 123 S. 18th St., Center City west, 215.972.8742; 12th and Spruce streets, Washington Square West, 215-629-9200. www.triacafe.com. Wine joins beer and cheese as the third of the trio of fermentables that give this bistro its name. Exceptional taps and bottles.

Vintage. 129 S. 13th St., Center City east. 215.922.3095. www.vintage–philadelphia.com. Weak tap list at this trendy spot on a no-longer-seedy stretch of 13th, but look for bottles of **La Fin du Monde, Victory Golden Monkey, Atomium, Westmalle Triple,** and **Stone Arrogant Bastard**.

> **"** In wine there is wisdom, in beer there is strength, in water there is bacteria. **"**
>
> —Anonymous

WINTER WARMERS

" Alcohol gives a false sense of warmth. **"**

—Alaska Department
of Labor warning

Well, duh—that's the basic idea behind drinking beer, isn't it? I mean, besides giving you something to wash down pretzels with.

Beer gives you a false sense of everything, from your ability to dance to the salient assets of the babe at the end of the bar.

But when it's 12 degrees outside and you've gotta trudge home alone because you struck out with that babe at the end of the bar, you miserable loser, who cares if it's "a false sense of warmth"? Drink enough beer, and you can convince yourself it's Miami Beach and you're soaking in a hot tub.

Yeah, with the babe at the end of the bar.

DRINK HERE

6 toasty joints with fireplaces:

The Black Sheep. 247 S. 17th St., Center City west. 215-545-9473. www.theblacksheeppub.com. Authentic Irish-style joint with a beautiful Mission-style fireplace. A neighborhood favorite.

The Dark Horse Pub. 421 S. 2nd St., Headhouse Square. 215-928-9307. www.darkhorsepub.com. An English-style pub where you can dry out after sloshing a yard of ale all over your chinos.

Gen. Lafayette Inn & Brewery. 646 Germantown Pike, Lafayette Hill. 610-941-0600. www.generallafayetteinn.com. The fireplaces are probably the oldest parts of the brewpub. The marble mantels are from the same stone in the fireplace that provided light to Jefferson when he wrote the Declaration.

The Plough & the Stars. 123 Chestnut St., Old City. 215-733-0300. www.ploughstars.com. On weekend nights, it's just another pickup joint. But huddle here on a quiet, gray afternoon and nurse that perfectly poured Guinness.

Rembrandt's Restaurant and Bar. 741 N. 23rd St., Fairmount. 215-763-2228. www.rembrandts.com. Wide-screen TVs, above-average tavern menu, darts, and **Stoudt's Gold** and **Philly Pale Ale** on tap, alongside a roaring fire.

Ten Stone. 2063 South St., Graduate Hospital area. 215-735-9939. www.tenstone.com. With a top-flight beer list (**Avery Hog Heaven barleywine, LaChouffe**), pool table, and darts, here's a fun way to make the wind-chill a nonfactor.

DRINK THIS

6 winter warmers, to take the chill off your bones:

Flying Fish Grand Cru Winter Reserve. Possibly the best value Xmas beer in Philly: great, strong flavor, very warming.

Riverhorse Belgian Frostbite. Your basic strong ale (8 percent alcohol), available with **Tripel Horse**, in the Jersey boys' Belgian Block case.

Sly Fox Christmas Ale. A nicely spiced (clove, nutmeg) red ale in a large (25-ounce) bottle.

Stoudt's Winter Ale. A delicious brown ale that's warm and perfectly satisfying.

Troegs Mad Elf. Extremely popular among beer freaks, it's a wine-like cherry-and-spice ale. Though it's available in 12-ouncers, it's always a treat when you find it on draft.

Weyerbacher Winter Ale. Malty and full-flavored, but not as overpowering as the Easton brewery's famous *big* beers.

❝ When I heated my home with oil, I used an average of 800 gallons a year. I have found that I can keep comfortably warm for an entire winter with slightly over half that quantity of beer. ❞

—Dave Barry

BEER GEEKDOM

For the truly impassioned beer drinker, the fanatic who bathes him- or herself in the culture of suds, *beer geek* is not a pejorative. It is a proud badge to be earned while sampling the local taps in a faraway town, to be worn on the sleeve while spreading the word among friends and family, to be shared among the fellow fans who invariably gather at famous beer haunts and festivals around the world.

A beer geek is someone like Diane Catanzaro, a college professor who writes beer haiku and named her cat Chimay, after the Belgian Trappist ale. Or John Ahrens, of Mt. Laurel, New Jersey, who was once listed in the *Guinness World Records* for the largest beer can collection (30,000 +). Or Ray McCoy, whose slogan is, "Life's a journey. Pack a cooler."

Beer geeks keep databases of every stout, pale ale, or porter that crosses their lips. They upload opinionated reviews at beer-tasting web sites, trade hard-to-find trade bottles by mail, travel the world, and worm their way into even the most private monastic breweries. They amass collections of rare, vintage beers and resist the urge to crack them open for decades. They are not snobs; they'll try almost anything, and they won't judge you harshly if you don't share their taste. You might call them obsessive; they say they're just having fun.

DO THIS

6 steps to total beer enlightenment:

Attend a beer dinner. Several area restaurants offer frequent beer-theme dinners, matching dishes with appropriate beers. Most brewpubs serve dinners featuring their own beer. **Monk's Café** (see www.monkscafe.com for schedule) organizes the most serious, bringing in out-of-town brewers and other celebrities. Other beer dinners served at:

Bridget Foy's. www.bridgetfoys.com
Eulogy Belgian Tavern. www.eulogybar.com
Old Eagle Tavern. 215-483-5535.

Go digital. Forget the pocket protector; what you need is a beer database on your PDA. You can track styles and proper glassware, and score all your favorites with custom software. 801-479-5390.

Go to school. Beer aficionado Peter Cherpack leads a five-week beer appreciation class at the Haverford Adult School. www.beerappreciation.com.

Learn food pairings. Tria Café sponsors a fun Fermentation School, with nighttime classes on various beer styles and how to match them with food. www.triacafe.com/fermentation_school.

Propagate your own yeast. Novices just buy a new yeast packet for each batch. The pros continue to grow new generations of their favorite strains, just like bakers who propagate yeast for sourdough bread.

Order beer by mail. Hard to believe, but some out-of-town beer doesn't make its way into Philly's beer distributors. But you can join beer-of-the-month clubs that will send a sixpack to your doorstep. Note: Pennsylvania laws officially prohibit beer sales from out-of-state sources, but some clubs have begun ignoring the ban.

> **Beer of the Month Club.** $29.95 for 12 bottles. 800-507-4660. www.amazingclubs.com/beer.
>
> **Beer on the Wall.** $20.95 for 6 mostly West Coast micros. www.beeronthewall.com.
>
> **Clubs of America.** $21.95 for 12 bottles. www.greatclubs.com/beerofthemonthclub.
>
> **Michael Jackson's Rare Beer Club.** Excellent selection of mostly large bottles of unusual beers. www.rarebeerclub.beveragebistro.com.
>
> **Micro Beer Club.** $31.50 for 12 bottles. www.microbeerclub.com.
>
> **World Beer Direct.** Nice assortment of clubs and different price levels, including international packs and high-end connoisseur picks. www.worldbeerdirect.com.

SHOW YOUR CHOPS

Wynkoop Brewing in Denver hosts the Beer Drinker of the Year contest each February. Candidates must submit a beer resume and, in a final showdown, prove their beer knowledge to a panel of judges in powdered wigs. www.wynkoop.com.

❝ They who drink beer will think beer. **❞**

—Washington Irving

CHAPTER **5**

Philly Beer History

TIMELINE

1680   William Penn receives a land grant and orders work to begin on a brewery at his estate in Pennsbury, Bucks County.

1683   William Frampton erects the first brewery in Philadelphia, along Dock Creek, Front Street between Walnut and Spruce.

1685   Samuel Carpenter builds a huge brewhouse on the waterfront. The site eventually expands into a full restaurant, the Tun Tavern.

1723   Ben Franklin arrives in Philadelphia, dines at the Crooked Billet.

1727   Franklin forms the Junto discussion group. Among its earliest topics: how to make better beer.

1728   In an early experiment, Franklin discovers beer warms faster in a black mug than in a white or silver tankard.

1734   Mary Lisle takes over her father's brewery at 2nd Street near Dock, becoming the first female brewer in America.

1756   Number of taverns in Philadelphia reaches 100. Population: 20,000, largest city in America.

1769 City brewers boycott shipment of British malt aboard the frigate Charming Polly and force it out of port, four years before the Boston Tea Party.

1773 City Tavern erected.

1774 Robert Smith begins brewing ale. His brand survives more than two centuries, till Schmidt's (which last owned rights to the name) closes in 1986.

1775 U.S. Marine Corps formed at the Tun Tavern.

1787 James Madison meets with delegates from Virginia and Connecticut at the Indian Queen Tavern, to devise key elements of the U.S. Constitution.

1795 Benjamin Rush of the Philadelphia College of Physicians publishes *Inquiry into the Effects of Ardent Spirits on the Human Body and Mind*, a treatise that denounces the intemperate consumption of spirits (but not beer). The paper spawns the American temperance movement.

1819 Frances Perot brewery on Vine Street installs steam engine, the first used to make beer in America.

1829 David G. Yuengling opens the Eagle Brewery in Pottsville, Pa. It's still operating today, as Yuengling Brewing, the oldest in America.

1840 First lager brewed in America, by John Wagner on St. John Street, Northern Liberties. (Historical marker at Poplar and American streets.)

1849 Engel & Wolf begins construction on a mammoth brewery at Fountain Green near the Schuylkill. It's the first of 11 beer plants that will soon transform the neighborhood into Brewerytown.

1860 The Bell in Hand opens near City Hall. It continues to serve beer today, as McGillin's Old Ale House, the oldest bar in the city.

Christian Schmidt, a 27-year-old German immigrant, buys Courtenay's Brewery in Northern Liberties, the start of an empire that will last the next 127 years.

1870 69 breweries in Philadelphia.

1876 Philadelphia Centennial Exposition features a Brewers Hall with the latest in beer-making technology. The city's largest brewer, Bergner & Wolf, wins the grand prize, but Frederick Pabst of Best Brewing wins a blue ribbon, later to be illustrated on countless cans of PBR.

First Mummer's parade kicks off more than a century of excessive beer consumption on Broad Street every New Year's Day.

A census counts 8,072 drinking establishments in the city, 3,782 of them connected to "houses of ill fame."

1919 Prohibition enacted. City shrugs, some breweries continue to operate for several years, many speakeasies open.

1925 More than 10,000 speakeasy operators busted in Philadelphia. Fewer than 10 percent ever go to trial.

1931 Philadelphia baseball fans at Shibe Park, weary of the Prohibition and near beer, boo President Herbert Hoover during the World Series and disrupt the game with a thundering chant, "We want beer!"

1933 Prohibition ends. Only the Poth brewery emerges from the score of plants that operated in Brewerytown.

1936 Crown Cork & Seal purchases the city's Acme Can Co. and begins production of the cone-top beer can, an early prototype. The company still operates near Manayunk.

1956 Massive Ballantine Beer scoreboard moved from Yankee Stadium, erected in right-center field at Shibe Park.

1961 State legislature passes law permitting beer to be sold in paper cups at Connie Mack Stadium.

1964 Esslinger brewery (10th Street and Callowhill) closes.

1987 Schmidt's, the last of the city's giant breweries, closes.

Stoudt's Brewing opens in Adamstown, Pennsylvania's first microbrewery.

1988 Samuel Adams Brewhouse opens on Sansom Street, the city's first brewpub. The site is now occupied by Nodding Head Brewery.

1989 City bans beer sales at Veterans Stadium after fans pelt players, coaches, and referees with snowballs during Dallas Cowboys game.

1995 Yards Brewing (Manayunk) opens and begins pouring cask-conditioned Extra Special Ale, the city's first "real" ale since the Prohibition.

1996 Copa Too pours Kwak on tap, the first Belgian draft beer ever poured in America.

1996 Red Bell Brewing opens at the former F.A. Poth brewery in Brewerytown. Files for bankruptcy three years later.

2002 Yards moves into the former Weisbrod & Hess brewery in Kensington.

2005 For the first time since Prohibition, Pennsylvania permits beer distributors to open on Sundays.

2006 Brewers nationwide honor Franklin with a special ale based on his early recipe for spruce-flavored beer.

COLONIAL TAVERNS

You know what's missing from this town's hokey horse-and-carriage, flag-waving, George-Washington-slept-here, Benjamin-Franklin-look-alike, ye-olde-tourist-trap trade?

Booze!

Did you know, for instance, that when William Penn arrived here in 1682, he likely stepped off his boat and directly into the city's first pub, the Blue Anchor Tavern? That means drunks have been stumbling around Philadelphia's cobblestone streets for more than 300 years.

Yet the local tourist industry virtually ignores our proud history of alcohol consumption and instead promotes corny Colonial tales of kite flying and flag sewing.

I blame this on the Quakers. Or perhaps the LCB (Liquor Control Board).

In any case, it's time to put the spirits back into 1776.

6 notable colonial taverns:

The Blue Anchor. Front Street and Dock Creek. Est. 1670. The original inn was an Irish pub that had been shipped to Philadelphia and reassembled right on the wharf. William Penn stepped off his ship, *Welcome*, and, as tradition has it, ate his first meal in his "greene countrie towne" here. For years, the city tried to have it torn down to make way for Front Street, and it eventually earned a reputation for rowdiness.

What's there now: Sheraton Society Hill.

The Crooked Billet. On the Delaware at the bottom of Chestnut Street. Franklin wrote in his autobiography that, on his first day in town at the age of 17:

> I met a young Quaker man, whose countenance I lik'd, and, accosting him, requested he would tell me where a stranger could get lodging. We were then near the sign of the Three Mariners. "Here," says he, "is one place that entertains strangers, but it is not a reputable house; if thee wilt walk with me, I'll show thee a better." He brought me to the Crooked Billet in Water-street. Here I got a dinner; and, while I was eating it, several sly questions were asked me, as it seemed to be suspected from my youth and appearance, that I might be some runaway.

What's there now: I-95.

The Indian King. Market Street east of 3rd. One of the largest pre-Revolution public buildings in America, it was the meeting place of Ben Franklin's discussion group, the Junto. The Brits took it over during occupation, mainly because of the size of its kitchen. "Though this house is one of the greatest businesses in its way in the whole city," one visitor wrote, "everything is transacted with the utmost regularity and decorum."

What's there now: Regent Shoes.

The Indian Queen. 4th and Chestnut streets. Before he moved to the Graff House (7th and Market streets), Thomas Jefferson bunked here on the second floor and started work on the Declaration of Independence. Years later, Gen. Lafayette recuperated here from wounds suffered at the Battle of Princeton. The vigilante Paxton

Boys, notorious anti-Indian backwoodsmen, once visited and shot up the adjoining stables.

What's there now: Omni Hotel.

The Old Plough. 2nd and Pine streets. Located just off the old Second Street market (now Headhouse Square), it attracted farmers and merchants.

What's there now: The Artful Dodger.

The Tun Tavern. East of Front Street at Carpenters Wharf, between Walnut and Chestnut streets. Est. 1685. Originally a waterfront brewhouse, it was one of the early anchors of Philadelphia daily life. It was the first meeting place of the city's Masonic Lodge; Benjamin Franklin organized the Pennsylvania militia in its rooms; and, most famously, it is the birthplace of the U.S. Marine Corps, on November 10, 1775.

What's there now: I-95.

STILL STANDING

George Washington (or one of his pals) drank here:

Broad Axe Tavern. Skippack and Butler pikes, Whitpain. Est. 1681. Possibly the oldest tavern in America, it opened before Penn arrived in Pennsylvania, more than 100 years before the U.S. Constitution was drafted. Though the building that houses the White Horse Tavern in New York is eight years older, that tavern didn't get its license until 1687. Broad Axe has been closed for a few years, but there are plans to reopen, possibly as a beer bar.

City Tavern. 138 S. 2nd St., Old City. 215-413-1443. Est. 1773. Founded by wealthy citizens and built through 25-pound subscriptions solicited among their friends, the tavern was intended for so-called "gentlemen." Washington met Adams here; Paul Revere spread the word of the British closure of the port of Boston in its dining room; and Franklin, Jefferson, and Hamilton all dined on its sumptuous meals. It burned to the ground in the 1800s; the current building is a re–creation of the original, built in 1976 for the Bicentennial. Enjoy **Thomas Jefferson Ale** and **George Washington Porter**, brewed for the tavern by Yards.

The General Lafayette Inn & Brewery. 646 Germantown Pike, Lafayette Hill. 610-941-0600. Est. 1732. During the Revolution, Lafayette manned the inn, then known as the Three Tuns, as an outpost to Washington's encampment at Valley Forge. In 1778, it was the scene of the fierce Battle of Barren Hill. It's undergone renovations over the years, but the unusual fireplace in the front bar is original. Today, it's a brewpub serving ceramic mugs of fresh ale.

General Wayne Inn. 625 Montgomery Ave., Merion. Est. 1704 as the William Penn Inn, it was renamed for Gen. (Mad) Anthony Wayne, who stayed here on his way to the colonial army encampment at Valley Forge in 1777. It's said to be haunted by the ghost of a Hessian soldier killed in the wine cellar. More recently, it was the scene of a grisly murder, when one of its owners shot his partner in a third-floor office. It's been sold and, at press time, was undergoing renovations.

Piper Tavern. Rt. 413 and Dark Hollow Rd., Pipersville. 215-766-7100. Est. 1759. Founded as a Bucks County crossroads inn, it was run by a Revolution army colonel, but it was his wife, Eva Piper, who was probably better known. Legend has it she faced down the notorious outlaw Doan Brothers with a boot full of buckwheat batter. She also helped finance the Continental Army with gold she'd inherited. Gen. Anthony Wayne, Franklin, Gov. Thomas Mifflin, and Stephen Girard all slept here. **Flying Fish, River Horse** on tap.

Standard Tap. 901 N. 2nd St., Northern Liberties. 215-238-0630. Though it has a woodsy, old-time look, the tap is 20th century. But it likely stands on the remnants of the 18th-century **Bull's Head Inn.** Author Peter Thompson writes that the Bull's Head was known for freak entertainment, including one show in which the owner invited drinkers to view a "wonderful" female child with "two heads, four arms, four legs, etc."

TODDLING TORISTOS

▶ A quick primer on the colonial beer scene can be enjoyed through Once Upon a Nation's terrific **Tippler's Tour.** It's a walk through Old City with a lecture on the importance of taverns in pre-Revolution Philly, with refreshing layovers at a handful of local pubs. Tours leave from the Independence Living History Center. 3rd and Chestnut streets, Old City. 215-629-4026.

Established in 1759, the **Man Full of Trouble** is the only original colonial tavern still standing in the city. It was built along the now-underground Dock Creek where it operated as a working-class pub, the kind of place that sailors and dockhands would've patronized before, during, and after a long day's toil. It's been owned by the University of Pennsylvania since 1994, but the school has unfortunately kept it shuttered and closed to the public, so BYOB. 127 Spruce St., Society Hill.

MY FAVORITE BEERS

TOM PETERS ▶ co-owner of Monk's Café, names the top 6 beers aging in his private stash:

 1. One last bottle of **1984 Chimay Grand Cru**, which I brought back from my first trip to Belgium. I'll share that with my daughter when she reaches legal drinking age. Isabel is 11 now.

2. At least one bottle from **every vintage of Thomas Hardy**. Some day I will do a vertical tasting (or should that be horizontal?) with a few friends.

3. A couple of cases of **Russian River's first batch of both Temptation and Supplication**. I'll be tasting a bottle every six months to see how well they are cellaring. So far, so very good. Supplication is one of my top 5 beers of all time.

4. A couple of bottles of **De Dolle Stille Nacht Reserva 2000**, which was aged in Bordeaux casks for two years. That beer is so f'n good, I share this with an occasional visiting brewer. I last popped one a couple of weeks ago to share with Michael Jackson and it was in stellar shape.

5. A **35-year-old Cantillon Gueuze** gathering a thick layer of dust. I just sampled a 1976 Cantillon Gueuze at the brewery in Brussels in September 2006. It was fantastic. Lots of citrus, that house-character barnyard nose and taste, and it finished bone dry.

6. Six small wooden casks of **J.W. Lees Harvest Ale** that have been aged with Lagavulin, Calvados, sherry, and port. They've been down there for several years. I'm thinking that we'll broach all those casks one night soon.

► A number of 18th-century taverns throughout the region are still standing and open for tours, including:

The Barns-Brinton House. 630 Baltimore Pike, Chadds Ford. $3 admission. 610-388-7376. Est. 1714. It operated as William Barns's Tavern in the 1720s, mainly as a roadhouse along the highway to Maryland. Though it doesn't serve beer, you can grab a bottle of wine next door at the Chaddsford Winery.

The Indian King Tavern. 233 Kings Highway East, Haddonfield, N.J. 856-429-6792. Yes, it's a dry town, but here you'll find the region's best look at colonial tavern life. This inn, established in 1750, was the emergency meeting place of the New Jersey legislature during British occupation of Trenton, and it was in its second-floor meeting room that the Declaration of Independence was ratified by the assembly. The building boasts labyrinthine beer cellars (not open to the public), authentic reproduction furniture, and colonial-era pageantry.

Stagecoach Tavern. 4 Yardley Ave., Fallsington. Guided tours: $5. 215-295-6567. Est. 1793. Originally the home of shoemaker John Merrick, the building operated as an inn from 1799 until Prohibition. It's part of Historic Fallsington, a Bucks County collection of preserved 18th-century buildings.

FRANKLIN AND BEER

❝ I doubt not but *moderate Drinking* has been improv'd for the Diffusion of Knowledge among the ingenious Part of Mankind, who want the Talent of a ready Utterance, in order to discover the Conceptions of their Minds in an entertaining and intelligible Manner. ❞

—Ben Franklin

Franklin himself practiced that "diffusion of knowledge" over a stein or two of beer. His famous Junto, a group of intellectuals who gathered to discuss the issues of the day, met regularly at the Indian King Tavern, near 3rd and Market streets. (And often the topic of discussion was how to make better beer!)

Yet, while benefiting from the social lubrication of these institutions, Franklin was a leading proponent of shutting them down.

At least, the ones that didn't meet his standards.

In the early 1740s, the city saw a rapid growth of so-called "tippling houses," or unlicensed drinking establishments, which catered mainly to underclass residents and slaves. An area south of Race Street had gotten so rowdy, it had become known as "Helltown."

As chairman of a grand jury that looked into the mess, according to Peter Thompson's *Rum Punch & Revolution: Taverngoing and Public Life in Eighteenth–Century Philadelphia* (University of Pennsylvania Press, 1998), Franklin declared that rather than diffusing knowledge, tippling houses were "nurseries of vice and debauchery," where one regularly heard "profane language, horrid oaths and imprecations."

BEN SAID . . .

"There are more old drunkards than old doctors."

"He that drinks his Cyder alone, let him catch his Horse alone. "

"He that drinks fast, pays slow."

"Drink does not drown Care, but waters it, and makes it grow faster. "

"Beer is living proof that God loves us and wants us to be happy."

"There can't be good living where there is not good drinking."

"Eat not to dullness; drink not to elevation."

"Nothing more like a Fool than a drunken Man."

THE DRINKER'S DICTIONARY

Though Franklin drank alcohol, he was a nag when it came to drunkenness. In 1736, he compiled a dictionary, "gather'd wholly from the modern Tavern-Conversation of Tiplers," with nearly 250 synonyms for being shit-faced.

Among my favorites:

A
He's Afflicted.

B
He's Biggy.
Been at Barbados
Piss'd in the Brook
Has Stole a Manchet out of the
    Brewer's Basket
Has drank more than he has bled

C
Half Way to Concord
Got Corns in his Head
He's in his Cups.
He's been too free with the
    Creature.

D
He's Disguiz'd.
He's seen the Devil.

E
He's Eat a Toad & half for Breakfast.

F
Owes no Man a Farthing
His Flag is out.

H
Top Heavy
Hammerish
Knows not the way Home

I
Lappy

M
He sees two Moons.

N
He's eat the Cocoa Nut.
Nimptopsical

O
Oxycrocium

P
Priddy
Been among the Philistines
He's contending with Pharaoh.
He's Polite.

R
He's Rocky.
Rich
Ragged
Been too free with Sir Richard
Like a Rat in Trouble

S
In the Sudds
Seen the yellow Star
As Stiff as a Ring-bolt
His Shoe pinches him.
He carries too much Sail.
Stubb'd
Soak'd
Has Sold his Senses

V
He makes Virginia Fence.
Got the Indian Vapours

W
The Malt is above the Water.

DEFUNCT BREWERIES

You walk the streets of the old neighborhoods, and sooner or later you start to hear the sounds of a city's forgotten past. Buried like 300-year-old cobblestones 'neath layers of asphalt, the ghosts are still alive...if you know where to look, if you know how to listen.

In Fairmount, you hear the creaking of a wooden wagon wheel coming down Poplar Street. In Northern Liberties, it's the tapping of a barrel-maker's hammer in the basement of a brick warehouse at 4th and Brown. In Germantown, it's a whistling steam engine that heats a brew kettle.

Smell the air—it's sweet with boiling malt and leafy hops.

The aroma stirs just the hint of a memory of a day when Philadelphia was the beer-making capital of America, when more than 90 brewers produced gallons and gallons of porters and lagers and ales. Beer made Philadelphia—not Milwaukee—famous.

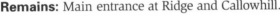

GHOST BREWERIES

Closed for years, these hulking, crumbling old breweries still stand:

City Park. 29th and Parrish streets, Brewerytown. 1857–1915. One of the city's best–known breweries (operated by beer baron Louis Bergdoll), it's now condo space. **Remains**: brew house, ice house, stables.

Esslinger. 911 Callowhill St., Brandywine. 1879–1964. Survived longer than any 19th–century brewery, except Schmidt's and Ortlieb's. Its mascot, the "Little Man," was a popular icon. **Remains:** Main entrance at Ridge and Callowhill.

F.A. Poth. 31st and Jefferson Streets, Brewerytown. 1865–1936. For several years in the late '90s before its collapse, Red Bell brewed here. **Remains:** wagon house, storage and fermentation rooms.

J&P Baltz. 31st and Thompson streets, Brewerytown. 1851–1920. Baltz tried to survive Prohibition by brewing Balto near beer. **Remains:** On Baltz Street, the small rowhouses were for brewery workers; also buildings for wagon works and shed.

Ortlieb's. 3rd and Poplar streets, Northern Liberties. 1879–1981. Henry Ortlieb, the great grandson of founder Trupert Ortlieb, ran a modern brewpub in the bottling plant for a few years in the '90s, before bankruptcy. **Remains:** In addition to the bottling plant, the old company tavern is occupied by Ortlieb's Jazzhaus.

Weisbrod & Hess. 2439 Amber St., Kensington. 1882–1938. Nearly everyone in this rundown section of Kensington forgot it was even a brewery, until Yards reopened the plant (on a much smaller scale) in 2002. **Remains:** The old horse stables, a crumbling power plant smokestack, tiled W&H logos.

EMPTY GLASSES I

Pre-Prohibition brews sound much like today's micros:

Bergner & Engel Tannhauser. Grand champion, 1876 Centennial.

Betz Brown Stout. "Invalids of both sexes requiring a gentle and strengthening tonic will find this an invaluable remedy."

Jacob Hornung White Bock. International Award for excellence, Paris Exposition, 1912.

Robert Smith India Pale Ale. Its namesake was trained at Bass Brewery before immigrating to Philadelphia.

Weisbrod & Hess Shakespeare Ale. Slogan: "The taming of the brew."

Wm. Massey's XX Ale. In the mid-1800s, it was sold from Maine to Louisiana, and exported to South America.

EMPTY GLASSES II

Old-timers remember these post-Prohibition lagers:

Famous Manayunk. From Liebert & Obert.

Gretz Pilsener. The family runs a distributor in Norristown.

Hohenadel Doppelbrau. On tap or by the bottle, just say, "I'll have a Hohenadel!"

Ortlieb's. Everybody in Philly drank Joe's beer.

Prior Double Dark. Originally from Adam Scheidt Brewing in Norristown, later brewed by Schmidt's.

Schmidt's. Some locals called it "headache beer," but it beat Coors in a highly publicized taste test. Today's bastardized version is a totally different recipe brewed for Pabst by Miller.

THE AFTERLIFE

Schmidt's of Philadelphia may be gone forever, but its yeast lives on in several commercially available beers, including **Victory Throwback Lager, Wind River Light Lager,** and **Russian River Blind Pig**, Want to make your own Schmidt's knockoff? Order North American Lager Yeast No. 2272 from Wyeast Laboratories, Inc. 541-354-1335. www. wyeastlab.com.

SING ALONG

Schmidt's is a dry beer, a mellow beer, a hearty beer,

Blended into one beer, a light, bright, fun beer,

Schmidt's...One beautiful beer!

—Schmidt's jingle

REFILLED GLASSES

6 modern beers recreated from old-time recipes:

Chateau Jiahu. This specialty from Dogfish is ancient. Its recipe is based on DNA tests of 9,000-year-old pottery jars found in Northern China. Contains fermented rice, honey, and fruit, and it's delicious.

George Washington Tavern Porter. A dark beer from Yards made with molasses. After the Revolution, Washington singled out Philadelphia porter as he urged the new nation to "buy American."

Poor Richard's Tavern Spruce Ale. Ol' Ben Franklin fiddled around with an old recipe for spruce-flavored beer. Dozens of breweries nationwide made their own version to celebrate his 300th birthday in 2006. Yards bottles its brew as part of its **Ales of the Revolution** package.

Stegmaier Brewhouse Bock. Old World German lager, from an early 1900 recipe at Lion Brewing.

Thomas Jefferson Ale. A strong golden ale with honey and other ingredients from a recipe at Jefferson's Monticello estate. By Yards.

Throwback Lager. A classic, pre-Prohibition lager made with flaked corn and German malt, from Victory Brewing (draft only).

A WAY OF MAKING BEER WITH ESSENCE OF SPRUCE

Recipe by Ben Franklin

For a Cask containing 80 bottles, take one pot of Essence and 13 Pounds of Molases.—or the same amount of unrefined Loaf Sugar; mix them well together in 20 pints of hot Water: Stir together until they make a Foam, then pour it into the Cask you will then fill with Water: add a Pint of good Yeast, stir it well together and let it stand 2 or 3 Days to ferment, after which close the Cask, and after a few days it will be ready to be put into Bottles, that must be tightly corked. Leave them 10 or 12 Days in a cool Cellar, after which the Beer will be good to drink.

TAKE A TOUR

The Neighborhood Tourism Network hosts regular tours to Northern Liberties and Kensington, home of the city's early breweries. www.gophila.com.

ATTEND A LECTURE

Pennsylvania beer historian Rich Wagner leads frequent Saturday afternoon talks on the city's old brewing scene at the Yards Brewery. Sip a brew and get the lowdown on Schmidt's, Ortlieb's, and other famous labels from the past. www.pabreweryhistorians.tripod.com.

PHILADELPHIA BEER

A 19th-Century Recipe for a Generic Philly Ale

Take 30 gallons of water, brown sugar 20 lbs., ginger root bruised $1/4$ lb., cream tartar $1^1/4$ lb., carbonate of soda 3 ounces, oil of lemon 1 teaspoonful, put in a little alcohol, the white of 10 eggs well beaten, hops 2 ounces, yeast one quart. The ginger root and hops should be boiled for 20 or 30 minutes in enough of the water to make all milk warm; then strain into the rest, and the yeast added and allowed to work itself clear as the cider and bottled.

From *Young's Demonstrative Translation of Scientific Secrets; Or A Collection Of Above 500 Useful Receipts On A Variety of Subjects* by Daniel Young, 1861.

PHILLY FACT

Wealthy Philadelphia brewery scion Grover Cleveland Bergdoll was one of the most notorious draft dodgers of World War I, fleeing to Germany at the start of the war. When he finally returned to America in 1939, he was immediately jailed and spent all of World War II behind bars.

OLD-TIME BARS

Thirsty for a quaff in an authentic, old tavern? Prohibition wiped out much of Philadelphia's pub history, but a few old bars from the 19th century still survive as vital drinking spots.

Among the most interesting is McGillin's Old Ale House, which claims to be the city's oldest continuously operating tavern. And who can argue? Opened in 1860, it's older than Wanamaker's, City Hall, and the Union League. Dark wood paneling and a large seating area give it a friendly beer-hall feel. It features a full, inexpensive menu and a fine selection of regional craft brews.

"When you come in here, you're standing on a 100-year-old tile floor. Our customers kind of appreciate our flaws." says the owner, Chris Mullins.

McGILLIN'S OLD ALE HOUSE

1310 Drury St., City Hall area   215-735-5562
Web: www.mcgillins.com

Drury Street looks like a forbidding Center City block, but it's part of a burgeoning neighborhood—renamed Midtown Village—that has seen a quick spurt of growth in the past five years. Don't worry about the lack of pedestrians—everyone's inside McGillin's.

Decorated with its original, 19th-century liquor licenses, the bar has been a favorite lunchtime spot since the Civil War, when it was called The Bell in Hand. Over the years, its patrons have included Will Rogers, John Barrymore, Tennessee Williams, Ethel Merman, Robin Williams, and Ed Bradley.

Today, it pours a nice range of area microbrews and serves a very affordable menu.

DRINK HERE

Step back to a long-gone era at these 6 pre-WWII beauties:

Cherry Street Tavern. 129 N. 22nd St., Logan Sq. 215-561-5683. Talk about convenience for the working man, there's a trough at your feet and a kitchen right in the bar. Order an egg salad on a star roll with a **Dogfish Head 60 Minute IPA**.

Grace Tavern. 2229 Gray's Ferry Ave., Schuylkill. 215-893-9580. The new owners of this handsome neighborhood taproom, operating since 1933, wisely left the tin ceiling and the Tommy McDonald–era Ballantine Beer sign from the days when it was known as Kelly's.

Kelly's Logan House. 1701 Delaware Ave., Wilmington, Del. 302-652-9493. www.loganhouse.com. Established in 1864 as a hotel, this wood-paneled bar has been attracting beer drinkers since the days that they actually rode in on a horse. Among its former guests: Al Capone, Wild Bill Hickock, and John L. Sullivan. $1 drafts on Wednesday nights.

The Khyber. 56 S. 2nd St., Old City. 215–238–5888. www.thekhyber.com. Established sometime in the 1870s, it has closed and reopened several times over the years. But that mirrored back bar (and the pee stains in the men's room) are original.

Regan's Bar. 4149 Roosevelt Blvd., Summerdale. 215-744-0940. The guy with his elbows on the bar has been there since it opened in 1944.

Snockey's Oyster House. 1020 S. 2nd St., Queen Village. 215-339-9578. www.snockeys.com. Though it's been at this location only since 1975, this old-time oyster bar still has the feel of the original, which dates to 1912. Try the Oyster Stew and a **Hoegaarden**.

YOUR FATHER'S BEER

"You know what I had the other night, and it was really, really good?" said Joe, the man who holds the fate of my scalp in his hands. "A quart of Schaefer."

I nodded politely, of course, and not just because he was flashing a sharpened object toward my ears. In Fishtown, the barbershop is the source of all authoritative information. It is here that you learn who's out of work and who's getting lucky.

Still, this bit of news was distressing. Joe is a beer enthusiast, an industrial-lager convert who I presumed had given up the dreck. Last time I got trimmed, he was talking about California micros and Chimay, the Belgian Trappist ale. Now, suddenly, he was waxing poetic about the subtleties of "the one beer to have when you're having more than one."

He must have caught my grimace in the mirror.

"Hey, I still like those other beers," he insisted, "but sometimes it's nice just to have a good, old-fashioned lager."

Gulp. Was my barber going retro?

DRINK THIS

6 retro lagers:

Pabst Blue Ribbon. The mooks who drink this think it's the ultimate statement of cool.

Reading Beer. On tap only in downtown Reading, by Legacy Brewing.

Rheingold. It's back, and so is Miss Rheingold.

Schmidt's. In a 16-ounce can, of course, it's one beautiful beer (no longer made in Philly).

Victory Throwback Lager. A pre-Prohibition macro lager recipe with Schmidt's yeast and corn.

Yuengling Premium Beer. Not the Lager; that's too trendy.

6 joints that serve retro beer:

Bob & Barbara's Lounge. 1509 South St., Center City west.
  215-545-4511. The interior is a shrine to PBR. Order a can with a
  shot of Jim Beam for just $3.

Citizens Bank Park. 11th Street and Pattison Ave., South Philly.
  215-463-1000. In a mood for nostalgia? Ballantine and Straub's
  are in the concession stands and Jamie Moyer is on the mound.

The Fire. 412 W. Girard Ave., Northern Liberties. 215-440-8515.
  Located within spitting distance of the old Schmidt's brewery,
  Philly's one-time favorite lager is served in all three forms: on
  tap, in a bottle, in a can.

McGlinchey's Bar & Grill. 259 S. 15th St., Center City west.
  215-735-1259. Even when you're drinking a micro, this place feels
  like it's still 1975.

Ortleib's Jazzhaus. 847 N. 3rd St., Northern Liberties.
  215–922–1035. www.ortliebsjazzhaus.com. You won't find Joe's
  beer at the former Ortlieb's brewhouse pub, but this cozy, wood-
  paneled bar still has the feel of Philly, circa 1950.

Tritone. 1508 South St., Center City west. 215-545-0475.
  www.tritonebar.com. Where Bob & Barbara's feels real, this joint
  just across the street seems full of posers bathing in the irony of
  cheap beer.

❝ Heineken? Fuck Heineken! Pabst
Blue Ribbon, man! **❞**

—Dennis Hopper,
Blue Velvet

CHAPTER 6

Excuses
to Drink

FESTIVALS

In the region's goofiest annual beer festival, Nodding Head Brewery hosts its annual Royal Stumble. This hairy-chested, mano-a-mano showdown, featuring brewers in full wrasslin' gear, reflects the true spirit of Philly's craft beer scene: it's fun, it's in your face, and it tastes great....

Instead of attacking with pile-drivers, the brewers assault each other with their best half-keg of beer. The only rule: It must be under 7 percent alcohol.

Then the gloves are off. The taco bar opens, the salsa band starts jamming, and, in a mad afternoon of mass beer consumption, attendees—patrons and brewers—suck down their favorites like the place is en fuego.

The first cask kicked is declared winner.

DRINK HERE

6 off-beat Philly beer events; you just have to be there to understand:

► **EVERY FRIDAY THE 13TH**

Friday the Firkinteenth. Possibly the single-greatest cask beer event in America. More than a dozen breweries participate, each bringing a single, small keg (firkin) of real ale, served without artificial carbonation. Hoisted atop the bar, the kegs are cracked open, and the beer flows till the shoulder-to-shoulder crowd kicks them all. Held at **The Grey Lodge Pub**. www.greylodge.com.

▶ **FEBRUARY**

Love Fest. Victory Brewing expanded its annual Beerathlon to include couples competing in a variety of beery events, including the Running of the Mugs. www.victorybeer.com.

▶ **MARCH**

University of Pennsylvania Museum Tutored Tasting. The beer event that turned Philly into a serious beer town, it had been hosted by renowned British beer writer Michael Jackson for nearly 20 years. Others, including yours truly, will try to fill his shoes, but everyone knows the thirsty audience is really there for the outstanding samples served in the museum's cavernous Chinese Rotunda. www.museum.upenn.edu.

▶ **MAY**

Sly Fox Bock Fest. Taste a half-dozen different Sly Fox bocks while enjoying (yes!) a manic goat race. The winning goat gets Sly Fox's Maibock named in its honor. www.slyfoxbrew.com.

▶ **SUMMER**

Dogfish Head Intergalactic Bocce Tournament. Another one of brewer Sam Calagione's whacked-out ideas, this summertime event features 16 teams of beer-drinkers competing on the Milton, Delaware, brewery's world-class bocce courts. www.dogfish.com.

▶ **JULY**

Royal Stumble. Each year, it's a different pro-wrestling theme, so inevitably the raucous event devolves into accusations of under-handed shenanigans. Held at the **Nodding Head Brewery**. www.noddinghead.com.

DRINK HERE, TOO

6 great Philly beer festivals:

▶ **MARCH**

Celebration of the Suds. This huge, two-day fest at the Atlantic City Convention Center is haunted by an unfortunate number of mainstream brews (does anyone really need to "sample" a Michelob Ultra?). But the high-end imports are here, too. www.acbeerfest.com. **Philly Craft Beer Festival.** The city's newest festival, at the Philadelphia Naval Shipyard, with 45 regional breweries on hand. www. phillycraftbeerfest.com.

► SEPTEMBER

Canstatter Volksfest. An authentic Oktoberfest held at Northeast Philly's Canstatter Volksfest Verein, the oldest German-American cultural organization in the city. Lots of German beer, singing, oom-pah music, and dancing. Labor Day weekend. www.cvvphilly.com.

Sippin by the River. OK, beer shares the spotlight with wine, but this late-summer event on Penn's Landing is a blast. And you don't have to worry about missing the Eagles game; it's broadcast on a giant screen. www.sippinbytheriver.com.

► OCTOBER

Great Eastern Invitational Microbrewery Festival. This longtime festival, at **Stoudt's Brewing** in Adamstown, introduced the area to many of the original micros, and it's still going strong. www.stoudtsbeer.com.

Kennett Brewfest. Held on the streets of downtown Kennett Square, it's grown into the region's most popular festival because of the high quality of beer provided by breweries. Features a special Connoisseur Tasting where you get a shot at rare "one-offs" and other unique flavors. www.kennettbrewfest.com.

OTHER AREA FESTIVALS

► FEBRUARY

World Café Beer Festival. University City. www.worldcafelive.com.

► MARCH

Main Line Brew Fest. Malvern. www.desmondgv.com.
Philly Beer Week. Philadelphia and suburbs. A week–long bash celebrating America's best beer–drinking city. www.phillybeerweek.org.

► APRIL

Brewer's Plate. Reading Terminal Market. Center City. www.whitedogcafefoundation.org.

Manayunk Brewfest. Manayunk Brewing. Manayunk.
www.manayunkbrewery.com.

Split Thy Skull. Barleywine fest. **Sugar Mom's**, Old City.
215-925-8219.

▶ **MAY**

Brandywine Craft Brewers Festival. Iron Hill–Media.
www.ironhillbrewery.com.

▶ **JUNE**

Garden State Craft Brewers Festival. Aboard the US *New Jersey*,
Camden, N.J. www.njbeer.org.

Harrisburg Brewers Fest. Harrisburg. www.troegs.com/brewfest.

MY FAVORITE BEERS

JAKE CARLIN ▶ bartender, Dawson Street Pub

1. Theakston Old Peculiar. Very malty with hints of caramel; close to a Scottish wee heavy. If ever you are in England, hand-pump heaven!

2. Yards ESA. The king of American cask bitters; I still remember my first taste at the first Philly Craft brew fest in `94, I believe. Brilliant!

3. Lindemans Gueuze Cuvee Rene. Complex, with the dryness of a desert, like a true French Champagne.

4. Liefmans Gluhkriek. Served heated. The blend of cherries and the complex maltiness teases the palate and warms the soul.

5. Guinness Extra Stout. Different from draft, it is highly underestimated in its complexity. It is rumored that small amounts of duff batches are incorporated to produce its unique flavor. It introduced me to the world of good beer, at the age of 15.

6. Kostritzer Schwarzbier. Chocolate maltiness, yet surprisingly light.

Note: My choice, if it were sold for mass consumption: **Nodding Head 60 Shilling.** Ex-brewer Brandon Greenwood's gem is the best session beer in America, hands down!

► JULY

Brew at the Zoo. Elmwood Park Zoo, Norristown. mysite.verizon.net/vze6vr65.

BrewExpo State College. State College, Pa. www.scbrewexpo.com.

► SEPTEMBER

Jenkintown Brewfest. Jenkintown. www.jenkintown.net/brewfest.

Lehigh Valley Brewfest. Easton, Pa. www.lvbrewfest.org.

Ludwig's Garten Oktoberfest. Center City. www.ludwigsgarten.com/oktoberfest.htm.

► OCTOBER

Newtown Brewfest. Newtown. www.newtownbrewfest.com.

► NOVEMBER

Great Brews of America. Lake Harmony. www.splitrockresort.com/ beerfest.

DRINK HERE (OUT OF TOWN)

6 beer festivals that are worth the trip:

► MARCH

Zythos Beer Festival. Belgium's premier beer festival with hefty pours of all those Trappists, trippels, sours, and even gueuze. Sint-Niklaas, Belgium. www.zbf.be.

► JULY

Oregon Brewers Festival. More than 50,000 beer fans show up for the 4-day event in a waterfront park. Excellent chance to try out all those Northwest brews. Last weekend of July. www.oregonbrewfest.com.

► AUGUST

Great Britain Beer Festival. Known as the Biggest Pub in the World, it serves 450 different real ales in five days. London. www.camra.org.

► SEPTEMBER

Oktoberfest. Pure debauchery (that's why you're here) but savor the beer. Munich. www.oktoberfest.de/en.

▶ LATE SEPTEMBER OR EARLY OCTOBER

Great American Beer Festival. Four hundred fifty breweries, 2,500 different beers star at the world's biggest judged event. Denver. www.beertown.org.

▶ OCTOBER

World Beer Festival. Catch your breath after the GABF, then head directly to North Carolina for 150 world-class breweries at the Historic Durham Athletic Park (scene of *Bull Durham*). www.allaboutbeer. com/wbf.

BEER FESTIVAL ADVICE

Have a system. Get a program and decide which beers you'd like to sample first.

Bring something to write with. Guaranteed, you'll fall in love with at least one brew and, by the next day, forget its name. Then, for the rest of your life, you'll wander the streets asking strangers, "Yo, what's the name of that beer? You know, the reddish-tan one with the bubbles...."

Get your money's worth. 'Nuff said.

Eat food and drink water. Those small samples add up to a big wallop.

Use public transportation or bring along a designated driver.

Wear a beer T-shirt, the more obscure the better. They're great conversation-starters and, guys, I'm told the ladies dig 'em.

❝ Of beer an enthusiast has said that it could never be bad, but that some brands might be better than others. **❞**

—A.A. Milne

BILL CONLIN'S TOP 6 BARROOM BRAWLS

Daily News columnist Bill Conlin has been on the Phillies beat for more than 40 years, and more than a little of his inside baseball knowledge was gleaned in barrooms on the road and at spring training.

1. Paul Owens vs. Dickie Noles, 1981

I had just finished writing in my room in the team's Chicago headquarters, the Sheraton Plaza Hotel. I went to the hotel bar, appropriately named Tiff's, and joined Rich Ashburn, his oldest daughter, Jeanne, and a visibly agitated Owens (the general manager). He was glowering and pointing at righthander Noles, who was seated with three or four players. They had just been broken up minutes before, after Owens said something about Dickie's pitching that afternoon that set him off. I knew Dickie pretty well and went over to talk to him. "Hey, no matter what he said to you, that's the GM and you can't get physical with the GM." Unknown to me, Ashburn, or Owens, the night manager had already called the cops. I looked out a window near our table and the squad car had just pulled up at the entrance and two of Chicago's finest were walking rapidly into the lobby. Just then, Noles mouthed a silent "Fuck you" at the Pope. Owens bellowed, "Son of a bitch!" And pounded his fist violently on the table, which was cluttered with glasses, beer bottles, carafes, etc. I could see the cops coming into the bar just as his fist came down and the glassware went up. I thought to myself, "If those bottles come down, the Pope's in trouble." They came down. While Owens was led off to the Rush Street Precinct in handcuffs, the players spirited Noles to his room. Ashburn called the precinct and they said to let Owens sleep it off for a few hours. He and traveling secretary Eddie Ferenz collected Owens around 4 a.m. (Noles is now the Phillies substance abuse counselor and widely acclaimed nationally in that field.)

BEER-SOAKED EVENTS

A generation from now, when scholars attempt to explain the history of America—the greatest, most advanced civilization in one million years of mankind—they will point to the events that took place one morning in a packed arena on South Broad Street as the moment this blessed nation crumbled to its knees:

Wing Bowl. We are doomed.

This annual debacle is ostensibly an all-you-can-eat Buffalo wing contest.

But, for pure depravity, this event has it all: Big-busted women bouncing on a trampoline, projectile vomiting, a guy who crushes beer cans on his head, prebreakfast beer consumption, a near-brawl between a contestant and a judge, and a wrestling match featuring bikini-clad babes doused in hot sauce.

Journalistic accuracy compels me to report that no bearded ladies are present. However, there have been wrestling dwarfs and a live chicken.

DRINK HERE

6 Philly events that were made for beer:

▶ **JANUARY**

THE ULTIMATE MUMMERS COSTUME

Mummers Parade. The beer consumption starts on New Year's Eve afternoon, beneath I-95 in South Philly, the ad-hoc staging area for many of the marchers. It spreads up Broad Street the next day, through the crowd and then back down to Two Street until the last keg kicks.

> **Best place for a beer: McGillin's Old Ale House.** 215-735-5562. www.mcgillins.com. Less than a block off Broad near Chestnut.

Wing Bowl. They don't serve alcohol at this hour in the morning, but they don't need to: When the doors open at 6 a.m. most of the crowd is already well tuned.

> **Best place for a beer:** If you still have the stomach for a victory chug, at **Finnigan's Wake**. 215-574-9317. www.finnigans.com.

▶ FEBRUARY

Mardi Gras. For a while, Fat Tuesday on South Street ranked right up there with Philadelphia's greatest celebrations of depravity, attracting 50,000 revelers, mostly kids from South Jersey. It's actually civilized fun now (though that doesn't mean you won't hear someone yell, "Show me your tits!").

> **Best place for a beer: O'Neal's,** just off South Street on 3rd.

▶ MAY

Dad Vail Regatta. College kids in the big city for the weekend—even in this zero tolerance era, good, cheap beer has been known to make an appearance at one of the nation's premier rowing competitions. Grab a sixpack and watch from the quiet west side of the Schuylkill, or plow into the mass of humanity along Kelly Drive.

> **Best place for a beer: The Bishop's Collar.** 215-765-1616. www.thebishopscollar.citysearch.com. It's the closest tavern to the finish line.

▶ JUNE

Cycling championship. Biking and beer go together like, well, biking and EPO. Breweries sponsor teams, fans bring kegs, stud athletes suck down pints at post-race feasts. The annual Philly race sweeps past primo picnicking spots on Lemon Hill and the taverns of Manayunk. (A week later, another race cuts through downtown West Chester, near Iron Hill.)

Best place for a beer: Dawson Street Pub. 215-482-5677.
www.dawsonstreetpub.com. Go the night before the race, when
patrons head over to the Manayunk Wall (Levering Avenue) to
watch crazy cyclists race *down* the hill in the dark.

▶ SEPTEMBER – DECEMBER

Eagles tailgaters. An absolute Bacchanal, the scene in the parking
lots is excess at its finest. Some fans don't even bother to go inside the
Linc, it's that much fun outside. Just don't wear the opposing team's
jersey.

Best place for a beer: BYO.

BALLGAMES

When the Phillies play at Citizens Bank Park, the green, natural grass
isn't their only bow to tradition.

In a gesture that warms the hearts of longtime fans who remember the good old days at Connie Mack Stadium, the Phillies serve Ballantine Beer.

That's right; the beer whose familiar three rings—Purity, Body,
Flavor—stood atop the giant outfield scoreboard at Connie Mack still
flows in Philly.

Ballantine was the defining image of Connie Mack Stadium. Other
than the waves of green, green grass, the sight of that huge scoreboard
in right-center field is forever seared in the mind's eye…. With 10-foot
letters that proclaimed, "You get a smile every time," it loomed over
the field, almost daring sluggers to knock one over the top.

DRINK HERE

6 places to drink and watch the game:

Big 5. Among the city's college hoops venues, only the Liacouras
Center (1776 N. Broad St., North Philadelphia, 800-298-4200,
www.liacourascenter.com), home of the Temple Owls, serves
alcohol. No locals micros, though Yuengling and Sam Adams
have been spotted.

WHAT WOULD ROCKY DRINK?

In a 2006 online Q&A, Sylvester Stallone proclaimed, "No question about it, Rocky drinks Rolling Rock, especially in the 'pony' bottles...." In the original movie, though, Rocky drinks bottles of Schmidt's at the Lucky Seven Tavern.

Boxing. New Alhambra Arena (7 Ritner St., South Philadelphia, 215-755-0611, www.newalhambra.com) and Blue Horizon (1314 N. Broad St., North Philadelphia, 215-763-0500, www.legendarybluehorizon.com) both pour mainly Bud.

Citizens Bank Park. The best beer selection at any ballpark in America. Nearly every locally made craft brewery is represented on tap, plus a good bottle selection that includes hard-to-find Straub's.

Lincoln Financial Field. After listening to fans' complaints, the Eagles now serve bottled Victory, Yards, and others at a couple scattered locations. Expect long lines.

The minors. All of the area's Double and Triple A teams serve great beer. Look for the Flying Fish Pub along the first-base line at Campbell's Field (Camden Riversharks), 401 N. Delaware Ave., Camden, N.J., 856-963-2600, www.riversharks.com. The Reading Phillies (where a 21-ounce micro costs just $5) even host summertime beer fests at FirstEnergy Stadium's pool pavilion, 1900 Centre Ave., Reading, 610-375-8469, www.readingphillies.com. The Iron Hill Wilmington is right across the parking lot from Judy Johnson Field (Blue Rocks), 801 S. Madison St., Wilmington, Del., 302-888-2583, www.bluerocks.com.

Wachovia Center. 3601 S. Broad St., South Philly. 215-339-7676. www.comcast-spectacor.com. The alleged Red Bell brewpub is dead, replaced by the usual crap. Hunt around and you'll find **Victory HopDevil**.

DRINK HERE (AFTER THE GAME)

Where to trash talk, whether your team wins or loses:

The Draught Horse. 1431 Cecil B. Moore Ave., North Philadelphia. 215-235-1010. www.draughthorse.com. Don't be surprised if the

Temple Fight Song (T, for Temple U!) breaks out while you're downing a Yards. Just down the block from the Liacouras Center.

Lancaster Avenue. Most of the bars within two miles of the Villanova campus fill up after Wildcat games. Try the **Erin Pub** (610-527-5941), **Kelly's Tap Room** (610-520-9344, www.kellystaproom.com), **Brownie's 23 East** (610-649-8389, www.brownies23east.com), or **The Grog** (610-527-5870). **The Wild Onion** (900 Conestoga Rd., Rosemont, 610-527-4826, www.thewildonion.com) has a decent tap list.

McFadden's Ballpark. One Citizens Bank Way, South Philly (part of Citizens Bank Ballpark). 215-952-0300. Head here in the seventh inning when the ballpark taps shut down. Unfortunately, the beer doesn't measure up to big league standards, and the gorgeous Beer Tub Girls are just out of my league.

New Deck Tavern. 3408 Sansom St., University City. 215-386-4600. www.newdecktavern.com. Crowded and brimming with Big 5 braggadocio following Palestra games. For better beer, slide a few doors over to the **White Dog Café** (3420 Sansom St., 215-386-9224, www.whitedog.com) where pitchers are just 8 bucks (except weekends) between 10 p.m. and midnight. **Mad Mex** (3401 Walnut St., 215-382-2221, www.madmex.com) has an uncomfortable zig-zag bar, but good micros and imports.

“ There are 16 institutions of higher learning at the University of Pennsylvania— 17 if you include Smokey Joe's. **”**

—President Gerald Ford

DRINK OF CHAMPIONS

"We basically turned the trainer's room into a bar. There were spittoons, beer bottles, empty pitches, cups, ashtrays and pizza boxes laying all over the place. Krukkie had a big leather chair in there right next to the counter so he could rest his beer and cigarettes."

—Terry Mulholland, describing the 1993 Phillies locker room in *More Than Beards, Bellies and Biceps* by Robert Gordon and Tom Burgoyne (Sports Publishing, 2006).

Smokey Joe's. 210 S. 40th St., University City. 215-222-0770. www.smokeyjoesbar.com. It's a "Pennstitution" with mostly frat-boy crap on tap, though it does have a single spigot devoted to **Yards Philly Pale Ale**. Enjoy a pint while gazing at the Quaker memorabilia.

South Philadelphia Tap Room. 1509 Mifflin St., Newbold. 215-271-7787. www.southphiladelphiataproom.com. The nearest beer to the sports complex—and the best. Excellent local taps, very good bar food. On the Broad Street Subway, get off at Snyder and walk two blocks north.

PHILLY BEER-DRINKING SPORTS HEROES

6 of the finest from the city's ale–ing sports teams:

Dick "Turk" Farrell. Member of the Phillies' infamous Dalton Gang, known to duck across the street for a beer during games at Connie Mack Stadium.

John Kruk. Phillies first baseman who traded his uniform number (28) to reliever Mitch Williams for two cases of beer. Williams later went on to own his own bar.

Tim Mazzetti. In 1978, the Penn grad went from bartending at **Smokey Joe's** one week to playing in a Monday Night Football game the next. He kicked five field goals in the Atlanta Falcons's 15–7 win over the L.A. Rams.

Vince Papale. In a story made for Hollywood, the South Philly bartender earned a spot on the 1976 Eagles roster as a walk-on after an open tryout. Papale was a gonzo special teams member for Dick Vermeil, whose story was the basis of the movie, *Invincible*, starring Mark Wahlberg.

PHILLY FACT

Connie Mack Stadium's 60-foot-high Ballantine Beer scoreboard originally stood at Yankee Stadium. It was moved here in 1956. After that, announcer Chuck Thompson used to call every homer a "Ballantine Blast," followed by his trademark yell, "Ain't the beer cold!" Richie Allen is the only Phillie to clear it with a home run, on July 8, 1965.

Tim Rossovich. Eagles linebacker who once beat Cowboys tight end
Mike Ditka in a contest to see who could open the most beer
bottles with his teeth. Ditka conceded when Rossovich started
eating the glass bottles.

Bud Weiser. Bench player on the 1915 Phillies National League
pennant team.

BILL CONLIN'S TOP 6 BARROOM BRAWLS

2. Dick Allen and me vs. racist barfly, 1967

The Phillies were staying at the famous old Edgewater Beach
Hotel about five miles north of Wrigley Field. I walked into a
joint down a few blocks away called Mr. T's. No. 15 was seated
at the bar, drinking Jack Daniels over ice. Curfew was 1 a.m. It
was about 2 a.m. Dick was drunk, but not knee-walking. Ditto
moi. We had a couple of drinks and were talking ball. A guy at
the end of the bar heard the ball talk, recognized Allen at that
point and started ragging on African-American players. He
ended one tirade with, "The biggest trouble with nigger players
is they don't have any balls." Allen got up and started walking
toward the guy, who also stood up. Allen didn't need another
incident. I stepped in front of Dick and knocked the guy colder
than Kelsey's nuts. Allen knew the bartender and he said,
"Get the hell out of here. I'll handle this." It was a three-block
walk to the hotel. A half-dozen fire trucks went speeding past.
There was a large crowd milling in front of the sprawling hotel.
As we got closer, we could see that most of the ball club was
standing in front of the south wing, where all the National
League teams stayed. Manager Gene Mauch, in a bathrobe,
was working a Marlboro when he saw Allen, dressed in a
Nehru jacket, crossing the street with me. He laughed and
held up two fingers—$200.

TAILGATING

Beer drinking in the parking lots around the Linc before an Eagles game is a spectacle that everyone should experience at least once, with everything from huge, trailer-drawn kegerators to gourmet brews. Most fans, looking to show off their good taste, willingly share their suds.

Three warnings:

Drink out of a cup. Public alcohol consumption is illegal and cops will confiscate your beer if you're dumb enough to drink it from a can or bottle.

Expect a long wait at the port-o-johns.

Don't wear a Dallas Cowboys jersey.

DOWN THE SHORE

The Jersey shore, birthplace of some of America's most important cultural institutions (notably the Miss America bikini scholarship pageant and the death-defying Steel Pier Diving Horse) is also home to one of America's noblest beer-drinking innovations.

I refer, of course, to the old seven-beers-for-a-buck deal at Somers Point's Anchorage Tavern. This buzz-inducing bargain—no longer to be found, unfortunately—introduced thousands of teenagers to the wonderful world of mass beer consumption and concomitant suds spewing. Back when Jersey's legal drinking age was a mere 18 (which effectively meant 16 at shore bars), the 7-for-1 deal was a rite of summer.

Not surprisingly, the evolution of brew down the shore has since focused only on quantity, not quality.

DRINK THIS

Is there a better place to enjoy a cold one than in the sun, on the sand by the waves? Drink these straight from the bottle—just remember to bring a huggie to keep it cool:

Flying Fish Farmhouse Summer Ale. Grab a sub from the White House (2301 Arctic Ave., Atlantic City, 609–345–1564) and head to the sand below Albany Avenue (no tags needed).

Monk's Flemish Sour Red Ale. A delicious thirst-quencher, this tart Belgian ale is made especially for **Monk's Café**, available at area distributors. Excellent with a late-afternoon clambake.

Sly Fox Pikeland Pils. A light, crisp lager with a surprising kick of hops. Better yet, it's packaged in cans, perfect for your cooler.

Stoudt's Gold. Mellow and sweet, with a pleasant hops character. Pour this for your friends who think the Coors they serve in the casinos is real beer.

Victory Whirlwind Wit. Wheat beer should be savored in a glass, but you're too lazy to get out of your beach chair. Just don't forget the bottle opener.

Yards Saison. This is my go-to beer when it's 10 a.m. and the beach is still empty. Light, spicy, and a nice way to get a vacation day started.

DRINK HERE

When you're looking for something other than loud bands, tanned life-guards, and beach beauties:

The Doc's Place. 646 Bay Ave., Somers Point. 609-926-0404. www.thedocsplace.com. Small, tight draft selection includes LaChouffe from Belgium. Nice deck view of sailboats and herons on the bay.

Firewaters. Brighton Ave. and the Boardwalk (Tropicana), Atlantic City. 609-344-6699. Fifty taps and more than 100 bottles, served by Hooters girls.

Plantation Restaurant. 7908 Long Beach Blvd., Harvey Cedars. 609-494-8191. www.plantationrestaurant.com. Excellent menu with a decent draft list (**Chimay, Wolavers, Flying Fish**), worth the drive up to LBI.

Tun Tavern. 200 Kirkman Blvd, Atlantic City. 609-347-7800. www.tuntavern.com. Beautiful brewpub that doesn't take many chances with its styles. But the beer is quite drinkable and occasionally top rate.

The Ugly Mug. 426 Washington Ave., Cape May. 609-884-3459. The taps are nothing special, but this is a beer-drinking institution. The hanging mugs that face the ocean belong to deceased members of the joint's mug club.

W.L. Goodfellows. 310 E. White Horse Pike, Absecon. 609-652-1942. www.wlgoodfellows.com. A glorified TGI Fridays with decent taps (that have been known to go skunky). You're better off taking a look at that extensive bottle list before ordering.

TAKE OUT SHOPS

It's mostly 30-packs for the shore house fridge, but you'll find a few gems:

Avalon Liquors. 2258 Dune Dr., Avalon. 609-967-4121.

Circle Liquors. 1 MacArthur Circle, Somers Point. www.wineaccess.com. 609-927-2921.

Collier's Liquor Store. 202 Jackson St., Cape May. www.colliersliquor.com. 609-884-8488.

Gorman's Liquor Store. 3845 Bayshore Rd., North Cape May. 609-884-2884.

Joe Canal's Discount Liquor Mart. 3119 Fire Rd., Egg Harbor Township. 609-569-1133. www.joecanals.com.

WARNING

If a shore house visitor brings you a bottle of **Jersey Shore Gold**, give him the boot. It's a defunct contract brew and that bottle is old. It wasn't all that good when it was fresh.

WHERE'S EDDIE?

Perhaps the classic Shore bar was Tony Mart's on Bay Avenue in Somers Point. A huge red arrow pointed beer-drinkers to the joint, one of the first places to grab a cold one on your way out of dry Ocean City. On a busy night, it employed 36 bartenders. It's where Bob Dylan discovered Levon Helm & the Hawks (later The Band), and it was featured in *Eddie and the Cruisers*, the 1983 Hollywood tribute to rock 'n roll at the Jersey Shore. After Tony Mart's closed in the '80s, several nightclubs filled the location. It's now empty.

STILL STANDING

Despite a fire in 2006, the Anchorage Tavern (823 Bay Ave., Somers Point, 609–926–1776) is alive and well. The bar, built in 1874, has attracted everybody from Prohibition-era rum-runners to dazed-and-confused punk rockers. Today, it's a bit more sedate as a cozy restaurant with lots of memorabilia.

SAND IN YOUR BEER

Since Atlantic City OK'd beach bars a few years ago, at least seven casinos have opened up huge tiki bars and clubs right on the beach. Look for cold brews within eyesight of the waves at the Hilton, Caesars, Bally's, Trump, Resorts, Showboat, and Taj Mahal.

In Sea Isle, the Springfield Inn (43rd and the Boardwalk, 609–263–3522) is as close to the beach as it gets.

OTHER EXCUSES TO DRINK

Still need another reason to drink good beer? Pick one of these:

▶ **Because Matt Lauer can't be fully appreciated while sober.**

The Beer Factory opens at 6 a.m. 113 N. Fairview St., Riverside, N.J. 856-764-0340.

▶ **Because your mom won't let you play ping-pong in the den any more.**

Bob & Barbara's Lounge sets up table tennis tables every Tuesday night. 1509 South St., Center City west. 215-545-4511.

▶ **Because you've only got 50 cents in your pocket.**

That's all you need for a pint of **Yuengling Lager** during happy hour at **Chris' Jazz Café**. 1421 Sansom St., City Hall area. 215-568-3131. www.chrisjazzcafe.com.

► **Because the tarot cards say you will meet a tall, dark double bock.**

Someone named Angel offers psychic readings on Tuesday nights at **Cross Keys Pub.** 3710 N. Easton Rd., Doylestown. 215-345-8020.

► **Because you need something to cover that hole you punched in the wall.**

Several taverns host exhibits with affordable art and photography, including:

Dirty Frank's Bar. 347 S. 13th St., Center City east. 215-732-5010.

North Star Bar. 2639 Poplar St., Fairmount. 215-684-0808. www.northstarbar.com.

► **Because you want to hang out with the girls.**

In Pursuit of Ale (IPA) is a group of female beer-lovers who meet regularly at city taverns to enjoy cold pints and chat about their favorite topic. www.myspace.com/ipabeerclub.

► **Because you've only got 10 bucks in your pocket.**

That's just enough to drink all night at the **Khyber** on Open Bar Sundays. Of course, you better have enough left over to tip your bartender. 56 S. 2nd St., Old City. 215-238-5888. www.thekhyber.com.

► **Because you get to buy the beers when you roll a 300.**

Several upscale bowling alleys with decent bars have opened around town. North Bowl has the best tap list, with Stoudt's, Yards, and Troegs, and $2 cans of **Dale's Pale Ale**.

North Bowl. 909 N. 2nd St., Northern Liberties. 215-238-2695. www.northbowlphilly.com.

Lucky Strike Lanes. 1336 Chestnut St., City Hall area. 215-545-2471. www.bowlluckystrike.com.

Strikes Bowling Lounge. 4040 Locust St., University City. 215-387-2695. www.strikesbowlinglounge.com.

► **Because you need some place to wear your beret.**

Ortlieb's Jazzhaus hosts jazz-and-poetry sessions throughout the year. 847 N. 3rd St., Northern Liberties. 215-922-1035. www.ortliebsjazzhaus.com.

▶ **Because you have a bunch of $1 bills in your pocket.**

The **Penn's Port Pub** titty bar pours **Philly Pale Ale**. 1920 S. Delaware Ave., South Philly. 215-336-7033. www.pennsportpub. com.

▶ **Because you're not getting any younger.**

Get a free beer on your birthday at **Ray's Happy Birthday Bar**. 1200 E. Passyunk Ave., South Philly. 215-365-1169. www.thehappybirthdaybar.com.

▶ **Because you don't have a record player.**

BYOV (Bring Your Own Vinyl) to the **Sidecar Bar & Grille** on Wednesday nights and drink Yards for just $3 a pint. 2201 Christian St., Point Breeze. 215-732-3729. www.thesidecarbar.com.

▶ **Because you've been in a foul mood since Bush stole the election.**

Drinking Liberally, an informal progressive social group, meets every Tuesday from 6–9 p.m. at **Tangier.** 1801 Lombard St., Graduate Hospital Area. 215.732.5006. www.drinkingliberally.org.

▶ **Because *Snakes on a Plane* cannot be viewed while sober.**

The bar's open all night during Movie Monday at the **Trocadero Theater**. Just $3 gets you in the door, and the cover goes toward your first drink. 1003 Arch St., Chinatown. 215-922-5483. Info and movie schedule: www.thetroc.com.

CHAPTER 7

Amusements

DARTS

The Philly darts scene is widely regarded as one of the best in America, because of the high level of play and the number of taverns (well over 100) with boards.

If you don't already play, buy a set of darts (they cost under $20) and carry them whenever you go out to a bar. A quick game of cricket is a great ice-breaker.

PLAY HERE

6 great dart bars, selected by Philly dart legend George Silberzahn, author of How to Master the Sport of Darts *(Totem Pointe Books, 2004), www.howtodarts.com:*

Buffalo Billiards. 118 Chestnut St., Old City. 215-574-7665. www.buffalobilliards.com. An award-winning bar whose interior brick walls give it a rustic feel. There are three dart boards, a bunch of pool tables, multiple TVs, a lounging area, and two bars. The menu is a step above expected bar food.

Curran's Irish Inn. 6900 State Rd., Tacony. 215-331-8628. The kind of Philly tavern that gives taverns a good name. Three levels, multiple dart boards, shuffleboard, and arcade bar games. Music on Friday nights and an excellent menu.

Dark Horse Pub. 421 S. 2nd St., Head House Square.
215-928-9307. www.darkhorsepub.com.
Its three active dart boards
are supplemented by three
others available for
tournaments and other
events. There are four bars
on two levels, large–screen
TVs, and arcade games.

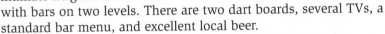

The Grey Lodge Pub. 6235
Frankford Ave., Mayfair.
215-624-2969. www.
greylodge.com. A more
intimate neighborhood tavern
with bars on two levels. There are two dart boards, several TVs, a
standard bar menu, and excellent local beer.

Jokers Bar & Grill. 7312 Castor Ave., Rhawnhurst. 215-725-6201.
www.jokersbarandgrille.com. A large sports bar with 12 dart
boards, pool tables, a boxing machine, and arcade dart machine.
It hosts Friday luck-of-the-draw night tourneys and a pro league.

Ten Stone. 2063 South St., Graduate Hospital area. 215-735-9939.
www.tenstone.com. An intimate neighborhood tavern with a
pool table, dart board, expanded tavern menu, and a wide
selection of beers.

WANNA PLAY?

The best way to improve your skills is to play in a league. Many area
bars sponsor teams. Each week, teams either play at home or on the
road, allowing you to discover new joints and new beer. Don't be
scared off if you're a newbie: Most league members are recreation
players and leagues are grouped by talent.

Delco Dart League. Lower Delaware County. www.delcodarts.com.
Old English Dart League. Mostly Center City. www.oedl.net.
Quaker City Dart League. The city's largest dart league, it mainly
plays in the river wards and the Northeast. www.phillydarts/qcedl.
Triple Shooters. American-style darts at **McNoodle's Irish Pub.**
7358 Frankford Ave., Mayfair. 215-624-9409.
www.tripleshootersdartleague.com.
Women of Philadelphia English Dart League. Northeast Philly,
Fishtown. www.phillydarts.com.

DART ETIQUETTE

Never walk between a player on the line (the *oche*, rhymes with hockey) and the dart board.

Never interrupt a player on the line.

Don't laugh at a player's shots.

To get into a game, check to see if there is a signup queue. Look for a chalkboard with names.

Remove your own darts from the board.

PHILLY FACT

The first dart board in America was hung in 1906, at a Philly bar at Ridge Avenue and Nicetown Lane. The tavern owner was an English immigrant named John Pearson.

CAN YOU THROW BETTER AFTER A BELT?

Andy "The Viking" Fordham, a 420-pound professional dart thrower, is known to drink a full case of **Holsten Pils** to relax before a match. Darts pro Silberzahn notes that while all the academic research would seem to dispel the myth of booze-aided perfection, among the health benefits of moderate alcohol consumption is relaxation and lower anxiety. So, yeah, maybe a beer or two can help a person play better. Twenty-four, on the other hand....

" You can take darts out of the pub, but you can never take the pub out of darts. "

—Phil "The Power" Taylor,
12-time world darts champion

POOL TABLES

If it weren't for the fact that you have to put down your beer to shoot, 8-ball would be the perfect barroom game.

That, and the unfortunate tendency some have of placing said beer on the table, then splashing it all over the felt.

You only make that mistake once.

PLAY HERE

6 joints with decent tables:

Buffalo Billiards. 118 Chestnut St., Old City. 215-574-7665. www.buffalobilliards.com. Ten tables, lots of TVs, darts, two bars with good beer. It's the rec room of your dreams.

Charlie's Pub. 114 N. 3rd St., Old City. 215-627-3354. I always get a good vibe in this place, but that doesn't keep me from sinking the cue ball.

Cheers to You. 430 South St. 215-923-8780. The tables are upstairs, but make sure you grab something from the bar downstairs, with a surprisingly big collection of Belgians.

The Dive. 947 E. Passyunk Ave., Bella Vista. 215-465-5505. No bar that dares call itself a dive would be without a table.

The Green Room. 1940 Green St., Fairmount. 215-241-6776. Two tables, no waiting.

Tattooed Mom. 530 South St. 215-238-9880. Two pool tables, decent beer, and some of the most painfully hip people in the universe.

6 PHILLY RINGERS

If one of these local players wants to play you, exit immediately:

Karen Corr. The Irish Invader is the No. 2 ranked female player in the world. She plays at Pete Fusco's Family Recreation Center in Feasterville.

Corey Deuel. No. 2 in the U.S. Professional Pool Players Association, he perfected his shot in Philly.

Jimmy Fusco. The Philly Flash has the look of a high school math teacher and the steady hand of an assassin, especially when playing his specialty, One Pocket.

Matt Krah. The Delaware Destroyer showed off on ESPN in 2006.

Willie Mosconi. Born at 8th and Wharton in 1913, the greatest player in the history of the game (he once sank 526 straight balls) has been dead since 1993. But he's reportedly still haunting tables in South Philly.

Elmer Smith. The *Philadelphia Daily News* columnist has cleaned my clock more than once.

JOIN A TEAM

The city has a couple bar leagues for players that use a handicap system (like golf) to even-out the talent:

American Poolplayers Association. www.philly.apaleagues.com.
East Coast Pool League. www.poolleague.com.
TAP. www.tapleague.com.

INSIDER TIP

When pool shooter Steve Mizerak proclaimed, "You can really work up a thirst even when you're just showing off" in those old Miller Lite commercials from the 1970s, he wasn't kidding. It took him 181 takes over $8\frac{1}{2}$ hours before he made a trick shot that was used in the ad.

JUKEBOXES

You're sitting quietly at the bar, peeling the label and stacking your change, when a stranger puts a buck in the juke.

The digits flash and the laser lines up on the disc, and suddenly the whole place is transformed.

It could be Sinatra or the Clash or Sheryl Crow or U-2, it doesn't matter. Music makes a bar.

And it makes you wonder, what makes a great bar song?

Loud? Well, yeah, the Ramones go with a taproom like a shot goes with a beer. But a few easy chords of Frank on *Summer Wind* make me order another whiskey.

BASS FIDDLER

Well-known lyrics usually click, whether it's a happy sing-along like *American Pie*, or the sad refrain of *If You Don't Know Me By Now*. But, I swear, one more chorus of *YMCA*, and I'm going postal.

LISTEN TO THESE

6 great songs about beer:

Beer Run by Todd Snider. *"All we need is a ten and a fiver, a car and a key and a sober driver."*

Dona Nobis Beer by Full Frontal Folk. *"Push-up bras, pleather pants, painting our lips red. Good beer, good show. Heaven with a head."*

Gettin' Busy with an A-B Sales Girl. The Pain Relievaz from Dogfish Head.

House of the Gods by The Pogues. *"Singha Beer, don't ask no questions."*

In Heaven, There Is No Beer. *"And when we're all gone from here, our friends will be drinking all the beer."*

Schaefer beer jingle. *"The one beer to have, when you're having more than one!"*

DRINK (AND LISTEN) HERE

6 great jukeboxes, with great beer:

Doobie's. 2201 Lombard St., Graduate Hospital. 215-546-0316.
Most played: Hurt, Nine Inch Nails cover of Johnny Cash.
Best beer: **O'Reilly's Stout.**

Good Dog Bar & Restaurant. 224 S. 15th St., Center City west.
215-985-9600. www.gooddogbar.com.
Most played: Acadian Driftwood, the Band.
Best beer: **Stoudt's Scarlet Lady.**

The Khyber. 56 S. 2nd St., Old City. 215-238-5888.
www.thekhyber.com.
Most played: Everybody Knows This Is Nowhere,
   Neil Young & Crazy Horse.
Best beer: **Yards Chateau Kenso.**

Royal Tavern. 937 E. Passyunk Ave., South Philadelphia. 215-389-6694. www.royaltavern.com.
Most played: Love Will Tear Us Apart, Joy Division.
Best beer: **Piraat.**

South Philadelphia Tap Room. 1509 Mifflin St., Newbold.
215.271.7787. www.southphiladelphiataproom.com.
Most played: This Must Be the Place (Naïve Melody),
Talking Heads.
Best beer: **Saison Dupont.**

Standard Tap. 901 N. 2nd St., Northern Liberties. 215-238-0630.
www.thestandardtap.com.
Most played: Wakeup Bomb, REM.
Best beer: **Dogfish Head Raison d'Etre.**

NEW WAVE MUSIC

The old Wurlitzer Bubbler is long gone, and some day those familiar
CD stackers will be outta here, too. The newest thing in bar music is
the Internet jukebox, which downloads digital versions of requested
songs over phone lines. Though users have their selection of more
than a quarter-million tunes, inevitably it's Frank Sinatra that gets
played the most.

LISTEN LIVE

6 beer bars with live music:

Chris' Jazz Café. 1421 Sansom St., Center City west. 215-568-3131.
www.chrisjazzcafe.com. One of *DownBeat* magazine's 100 best
jazz clubs in the world, where the cover can be as cheap as
8 bucks.

Johnny Brenda's. 1201 Frankford Ave., Fishtown. 215-739-9684.
www.johnnybrendas.com. The recently opened second-floor
performance space (with balcony) is already one of Philly's
favorite spots for national and local acts.

The Khyber. 56 S. 2nd St., Old City. 215-238-5888.
www.thekhyber.com. Still the loudest, with punk, electric,
blues, jam—name it—along with excellent taps (and $2 PBR).

North Star Bar. 2639 Poplar St., Fairmount. 215-684-0808.
www.northstarbar.com. Everything from loud rock 'n roll to
alternative WXPN-ish acts. Make sure you grab a seat at the bar
for a stage view.

Ortlieb's Jazzhaus. 847 N. 3rd St., Northern Liberties. 215-922-1035.
www.ortliebsjazzhaus.com. Longtime owner/saxman Pete
Souder has sold the joint, but jazz continues—along with a tap
line upgrade. Drummer Mickey Roker leads the house band.

World Café Live. 3025 Walnut St., University City. 215-222-1400. www.worldcafe.com. Geared for the over-30 crowd, this is a kick-ass live music venue with a very respectable beer list, including Victory, Troegs, Dogfish Head, and more.

> **"** Well I woke up this mornin' and I got myself a beer. **"**
>
> —Jim Morrison

SHUFFLEBOARD

In any taproom, in any city, on any planet, those words— "Let's get an impartial observer"—should be singularly regarded as an immutable cue to duck. Vanish. Evaporate. Never, under any circumstances—even if the individual soliciting your help is your own dear mother—should a patron in a bar agree to act as "an impartial observer." You are not merely asking for trouble when you step up as an impartial observer, you are sending out an engraved invitation with a return address from Suckerville.

I know this. You know this.

Mark did not know this.

He puts down his pint and steps over to the shuffleboard table.

He's asked: "Which one's closer to the edge, red or blue?"

He leans toward the table, adjusts his eyeglasses, and squints.

He pauses a second. The spoon guy stops playing. I put down my glass. Mark utters the fateful word.

"Blue."

In a flash, the pub is turned upside down. A fist connects with Red's jaw. Barstools tumble to the ground. Beer soaks my shirt. I grab Mark by the shoulder and drag him to safety out on Lancaster Avenue.

We leave our pints behind, half full of Guinness Stout.

HOW TO PLAY

There are a variety of games with different rules, so agree on your game before starting.

The most common game is Knock Off, either singles or pairs. Flip a coin and decide who slides the weight first (going last gives you the strategic advantage). Take turns shooting. Only one team scores each round, with points for each weight that is closer to the end line than the opposing team's closest weight.

Score one point if the weight is between the foul line and the 2 line, two points if it's between the 2 and 3 lines, three points if it's beyond the 3 line, but still on the board. Hangers—weights that are hanging over the end line—are worth four points.

AREA JOINTS WITH SHUFFLEBOARD TABLES

Don't rest your beer on the table! Wet spots screw up the sliding action.

Casper's Lounge. 3510 Cottman Ave., Mayfair. 215-331-1717.

Cheers Café. 2601 E. Westmoreland St., Port Richmond. 215-426-9604.

Dave & Buster's. 325 N. Columbus Blvd. (Pier 19), Penn's Landing. 215-413-1951.

Duffer's Tavern. 192 Middletown Rd., Glen Mills. 610-358-5050.

Firkin Tavern. 1400 Parkway Ave., Ewing Township, N.J. 609-771-0100.

Gambol's Café. 3722 Garrett Rd., Drexel Hill. 610-259-2702.

J&C's Tavern. 6601 Lansdowne Ave., West Philly. 215-878-7343.

McCarron's First Inn. 5500 Torresdale Ave., Wissinoming. 215-289-2260.

McFadden's Tavern. 7319 West Chester Pike, Upper Darby. 610-352-9724.

McKenzie Brew House. 451 Wilmington-West Chester Pike, Glen Mills. 610-361-9800.

Sly Fox Brewery & Restaurant. 312 Lewis Rd., Royersford. 610-948-8088.

Wayne Beef & Ale. 232 W. Wayne Ave., Wayne. 610-688-2337.

PHILLY FACT

Shuffleboard was banned in Philadelphia in the early 19th century as an illegal public gaming. But in an 1848 court case, a bar owner argued successfully that shuffleboard is a game of skill, not chance.

BILL CONLIN'S TOP 6 BARROOM BRAWLS

3. Larry Colton vs. Ma Bell, 1968

The Phillies had a righthander named Larry Colton. His big-league career consisted of 2 IP, an 0-0 record, and a 4.50 ERA for his sole relief appearance. He was a player of some interest because he was the son-in-law of actress Hedy Lamarr. (He is now a published author.) Colton, who was 6-3, 230, and quite handsome, got into it with several locals at some meat market. In the altercation that resulted, Larry sustained a dislocated pitching shoulder. Back at the Jack Tar Hotel, Colton called trainer Joe Liscio and complained that his phone rang shortly after he went to bed. He was sleeping with his right arm away from the phone and injured it rolling over awkwardly and dislocated his shoulder. The Phillies actually tried to sell this fiction to the media. *Bulletin* beat man Ray Kelly Sr. had a classic line when Gene Mauch told the phone story to us with a straight face. "Yeah," Kelly cracked, "but the phone had a 250-pound bouncer attached to it."

QUIZZO

Unlike darts or 8-ball, Quizzo is the one bar game that requires absolutely no talent. That is, unless you think instant recall of obscure Simpson's characters is a talent.

The game, for the rare boozehound who hasn't encountered it yet, is a simple trivia quiz, with tables of patrons competing for small prizes—usually $50 or so toward your bar tab. There's no entry fee; just keep ordering pitchers and come up with a witty name for your team.

The quizzes aren't all that tough, though if the crowd is young the questions (Name the current No. 1 rap album in America) can make you feel old. But Quizzo isn't about the questions; it's about the guy or gal running the show. The best Quizzo hosts are as sharp-witted as a standup comic.

ANSWER THESE

Johnny Goodtimes, the city's best-known Quizzo host (www.johnny-goodtimes.com), offers these challenges:

1. What country's citizens drink the most beer per capita?
   a. Germany
   b. Ireland
   c. Czech Republic
   d. United States

2. What beer did Billy Dee Williams tell us "works every time"?

3. Who had a hit with the song *Strange Brew*?

4. Name the man who sang *What Made Milwaukee Famous (Has Made a Loser Out of Me)*. Hint: He's cousins with Jimmy Swaggart.

5. Name the famous Rudyard Kipling poem that begins:

You may talk o' gin and beer
When you're quartered safe out 'ere,
An' you're sent to penny-fights an' Aldershot it.

6. What blues legend originally sang the song, *One Bourbon, One Scotch, One Beer*?

ANSWERS 1. c. Czech Republic. Ireland is 2nd, Germany is 3rd, the U.S. is 13th. **2.** Colt 45. **3.** Cream. **4.** Jerry Lee Lewis. **5.** Gunga Din. **6.** John Lee Hooker.

DRINK (AND ANSWER) HERE

Weekly Quizzo games:

Dawson Street Pub. 100 Dawson St., Manayunk. www.dawsonstreetpub.com. 215-482-5677. Tuesday, 8:30 p.m.
Deuce Restaurant & Bar. 1040 N. 2nd St., Northern Liberties. 215-413-3822. www.deucerestaurant.com. Tuesday, 9:15 p.m.
Fergie's Pub. 1214 Sansom St., Center City east. 215-928-8118. www.fergies.com. Tuesday, 9 p.m.
Good Dog Bar & Restaurant. 224 S. 15th St., Center City west. 215-985-9600. Wednesday, 8 p.m.

Nodding Head Brewery & Restaurant. 1516 Sansom St., Center City west. 215-569-9525. Sunday, 8 p.m.

South Philadelphia Tap Room. 1509 Mifflin St., South Philly. 215-271-7787. Tuesday, 9 p.m.

INSIDER TIP

Who invented Quizzo? No one knows for sure, but the earliest mention of it in Philly newspapers is April 1994, in a column by former *Inquirer* writer Clark DeLeon. He wrote about a weekly trivia game at the old Mick-Daniels Saloon at 2nd and Snyder in South Philly, hosted by a guy nicknamed Mr. Quizo.

SPORTS BARS

You know the drill: Three thousand wide-screen HDTVs, a billion pixels, 48 concurrent games...and every one of 'em is in a commercial break.

WATCH HERE

6 joints with good games and great beer:

Dave & Buster's. 325 N. Columbus Blvd., Penn's Landing. 215-413-1951. www.daveandbusters.com. Big, loud, and manic, it's Chuck-e-Cheese's for SUV-driving suburbanites who complain about paying 10 bucks for a parking spot. Still, the TVs are plentiful and you can watch while shooting 8-ball.

Fox and Hound Smokehouse and Tavern. 1501 Spruce St., Center City west. 215-732-8610. Has all the charm of a hotel lobby in downtown Wichita, but there's no shortage of TVs and fine beer (Spaten, Dogfish Head, Legacy) among the 36 taps.

Just Sports. 600 New Rodgers Rd., Bristol. 215-781-9556. www.justsportsbarandgrill.com. Excellent beer selection (Troegs, Allagash, Victory, Stoudt's) served at a bar crafted from shuffleboard tables.

McMenamin's Tavern. 7170 Germantown Ave., West Mt. Airy. 215-247-9920. Classic neighborhood taproom with the perfect mix of beer, food, and Eagles fans. Sponsors bus trips down to the Linc.

O'Neal's. 611 S. 3rd St., South Street area. 215-574-9495. www.onealspub.com. South Street's best beer selection with the usual mix of area sports plus European football league action. Watch out for beer-chugging rugby players.

Whiskey Tango Tavern. 14000 Bustleton Ave., Somerton. 215-671-9234. www.whiskeytangotavern.com. A pair of 10-foot TVs, multiple bars, and La-Z-Boys, but the mainstream beer is what you'd expect from a joint just this side of Bucks County.

CHAIN GANG

Two area chains dominate the sports bar scene on either side of the Delaware.

In Pennsylvania, it's the insanely popular **Chickie's & Pete's Crab House & Sports Bar.** This is a Philly institution that deserves to be in this guide, even if it serves mainly BudMillerCoors. Its original site in Mayfair is the warmest, but others, listed below, host game-time events with area sports personalities that are often broadcast live on the radio. Its South Philly location, which runs shuttles to and from the sports complex, was voted the No. 3 sports bar in America by ESPN. It also serves **Victory HopDevil** on tap. Try one with the excellent crab fries. www.chickiesandpetes.com.

Locations:
4010 Robbins Ave., Mayfair. 215-218-0500.
11500 Roosevelt Blvd., Northeast Philly. 215-218-0500.
1526 Packer Ave., South Philly (near the sports complex). 215-218-0500.
183 Rt. 130, Bordentown, N.J. 609-298-9182.
6055 Blackhorse Pike, Egg Harbor Twp., NJ. 609-272-1930.

In Jersey, the go-to sports joint is **P.J. Whelihan's Pub**. Though I have an instinctive aversion to any place named with dopey initials, this joint deserves credit for a friendly atmosphere and a very good beer selection. Its house beer, **P.J.W. Copper Lager**, is made by Victory, and you should be able to find another two or three micros on tap, including **Allagash, Yards,** and **Harpoon.**

Locations:
1854 E. Marlton Pike, Cherry Hill, N.J. 856-424-8844.
700 Haddon Ave., Haddonfield, N.J. 856-427-7888.
396 Lenola Ave., Maple Shade, N.J. (near Moorestown Mall). 856-234-2345.

61 Stokes Rd., Medford Lakes, N.J. 609-714-7900.
425 Hurfville-Cross Keys Rd., Sewell, N.J. 856-582-7774.
799 DeKalb Pike, Blue Bell. 610-272-8919.
4595 Broadway, Allentown. 610-395-2532.
1658 Hausman Rd., Allentown. 610-395-4077.

REAL JOCK BARS

Looking for a joint owned by a pro?

Bergey's Sports Bar. 140 Moorehead Ave., West Conshohocken.
610-260-0064. That's Bergey as in Wings pro lacrosse player Jake
Bergey, whose dad is ex-Eagles linebacker Bill.

Larry Holmes Ringside Restaurant & Lounge. 91 Larry Holmes
Dr., Easton. 610-250-0202. www.larryholmes.com. Lots of photos
and the ex-heavyweight's championship belts.

INSIDER TIP

In the 1950s, one of the favorite nightspots for ballplayers was
the old Moon-Glo Supper Club at Juniper and Race streets in
Center City. It lost its charm in 1959, however, when Phillies
pitcher Humberto Robinson accused the owner, Harold
"Boomy" Friedman, of offering him $1,500 to throw a game
against the Cincinnati Reds. Robinson turned him down and
won the game; Friedman was sent to jail.

TAVERN GAMES

Air hockey. Not a particularly popular bar sport because innocent
bystanders just hate it when the puck lands in their mug.

Where to slap the puck:

Hollywood Bistro. 7400 Bustleton Ave., Roosevelt Mall,
Rhawnhurst. 215-722-4312.

Beirut or Pong. LCB officials look dimly on this drinking game, so
taverns don't advertise it. Look for it mainly in college bars.

Bocce. If it weren't for the space required, this would be the world's most popular bar game. Anyone who can hold a ball can play, and you never need to put down your glass. Dogfish Head Brewery in Milton is hoping to bring back its pair of outdoor courts when its ongoing expansion is completed. In the city, there are more than a dozen organized bocce clubs, some of which welcome new members and serve drinks.

Where to roll:

Bacco. 587 DeKalb Pike, North Wales. 215-699-3361.
www.baccobacco.com.
Chestnut Hill Bocce Club. 118 E. Hartwell Ln., Chestnut Hill.
215-247-9776.
Duffer's Pub. 996 Baltimore Pike, Concordville. 610-558-2122.
www.dufferspa.com.

Foosball. Possibly the most energetic of all bar games because it takes both hands to play. Remember: No spinning allowed! www.phillyfoos.com.

Where to foos:

Brownie's Pub. 46 N. 2nd St., Old City. 215-238-1222.
Buffalo Billiards. 118 Chestnut St., Old City. 215-574-7665.
www.buffalobilliards.com.
Druid's Keep. 149 Brown St., Northern Liberties. 215-413-0455.
McKenzie Brew House. 240 Lancaster Ave., Malvern,
610-296-2222; and 451 Wilmington Pike, Glen Mills,
610-361-9800. www.mckenziebrewhouse.com.
Walsh's Tavern. 63 York Rd., Warminster. 215-675-0149.
Holds tournaments every Monday night.

Golden Tee. An absolutely addictive and challenging video golf game that lets you play for prizes against other players across the country.

Where to spend your quarters:

Bethayres Tavern. 2231 Huntingdon Pike, Huntingdon Valley.
215-947-9729. www.bethayrestavern.com.
Chap's Taproom. 2509 W. Main St., Jeffersonville. 610-539-8722.
www.chapstap.com.
Fox and Hound Smokehouse & Tavern. 1501 Spruce St., Center
City west. 215-732-8610.
Rock Bottom Brewery. 160 N. Gulph Rd., King of Prussia.
610-230-2739. www.rockbottom.com.

Karaoke. Yeah, it's corny as hell. But get a couple good beers into your gut, and you'll be singing along with Journey, too.

Where to carry a tune:

Abbaye. 637 N. 3rd St., Northern Liberties. 215-940-1222. Sunday, 11 p.m.

Finnigan's Wake. 537 N. 3rd St., Northern Liberties. 215-574-9240. www.finnigans.com. Wednesday, 9:30 p.m.

Moriarty's. 1116 Walnut St., Center City east. 215-627-7676. www.moriartyspub.com. Saturday, 9 p.m.

The Wild Onion. 900 Conestoga Rd., Rosemont. 610-527-4826. www.thewildonion.com. Monday, 10 p.m.

Texas Hold 'Em. Gambling is still illegal in Philly bars (though the coming slot casinos will change that soon enough). Plenty of taverns, however, bring in crowds with weekly poker tournaments with nominal prizes.

Where to bluff:

Downey's. 526 S. Front St., South Street area. 215-625-9500. www.downeysrestaurant.com. Sunday and Monday, 8:30 p.m.

Fado. 1500 Locust St., Center City west. 215-893-9700. www.fadoirishpub.com. Tuesday, 8 p.m.

Fox & Hound Smokehouse & Tavern. 1501 Spruce St., Center City west. 215-732-8610. Thursday, 8:30 p.m.

Manayunk Brewery & Restaurant. 4120 Main St., Manayunk. 215.482.8220. www.manayunkbrewery.com. Thursday, 8:30 p.m.

McGillin's Old Ale House. 1310 Drury St., City Hall area. 215-735-5562. www.mcgillins.com. Thursday, 8 p.m.

Roosevelt's Pub. 2222 Walnut St., Center City west. 215-569-8879. Wednesday, 8 p.m.

The Philadelphia Poker League ranks area players. www.philadelphiapokerleague.com.

READING MATERIAL

You hear a lot of complaints these days about the lack of decent textbooks in our city's public schools. Ancient science books and graffiti-filled history books apparently have parents, teachers, and kiddies whining for more tax dollars.

Schools, schmools—speaking as the voice of the drinking public, I think it's high time the city paid a little more attention to the severe lack of decent books in our taprooms.

That's right, from corner bars to trendy bistros, the state of reading material has never been worse. Once, you could count on every tavern to own at least two irreplaceable texts:

> **The Baseball Encyclopedia**, to settle 90 percent of all barroom arguments.
> **Daily Racing Form**, for entertainment purposes only.

These days, you're lucky if you can find a beat-up copy of one of those city weeklies.

READ THIS

6 essentials for the tavern library:

The Bulletin Almanac. An old copy of the best Philly reference since Poor Richard's.

Guinness World Records. How else will you know whether your consumption of three dozen raw eggs is a record?

The New Limerick. An out-of-print book that contains more than 2,700 bawdy examples of the purest form of English literature.

The **Philadelphia Daily News**. Grab today's People Paper…and thanks!

The Pocket Guide to Beer (Running Press, 2000). Still the best collection of the world's beers, by the man who guzzled them all, Michael Jackson.

Trivial Pursuit cards. Break the ice with your complete mastery of useless knowledge.

SUZANNE WOODS ▶ founder, In Pursuit of Ale women's beer appreciation club, names some female-friendly joints:

1. Ray's Happy Birthday Bar. 1200 E. Passyunk Ave., South Philly. 215-365-1169. www.thehappy-birthdaybar.com. Charming owner, Lou Capp, will customize your experience on a Friday afternoon with gender-specific jokes.

2. Tria Café. 123 S. 18th St., Rittenhouse Square. 215-972-8742. www.triacafe.com. Beer list is classified by titles ranging from "Invigorating" and "Friendly" to "Profound" and "Extreme," guiding novice beer drinkers through their experience.

3. Johnny Brenda's. 1201 Frankford Ave., Fishtown. 215-739-9684. www.johnnybrendas.com. Live music, great local beer selection, and a pink paradise of a bathroom for the ladies.

4. Pub on Passyunk East (P.O.P.E.). 1501 E. Passyunk Ave., South Philly. 215-755-5125. Hooks for handbags!

5. The Grey Lodge Pub. 6235 Frankford Ave., Mayfair. 215-624-2969. www.greylodge.com. The women's water closet is a mosaic wonderland covered in quotes about love and money. Oh, and Ms. Pac Man will keep you young at heart.

6. Monks Café. 254 S. 16th St., Center City west. 215-545-7005. www.monkscafe.com. Belgians such as Monk's **Signature Flemish Sour Ale** and **St. Bernardus Abt 12**, although complex, have served as great gateway beers to women who might not know life beyond American light lagers.

DRINK (AND READ) HERE

6 joints where it's not antisocial to read:

700. 700 N. 2nd St., Northern Liberties. 215-413-3181. In the afternoon, sneak upstairs with a pint, to the vacant lounge that was once, believe it or not, my buddy Weg's living room.

The Khyber. 56 S. 2nd St., Old City. 215-238-5888. www.thekhyber.com.Grab a table by the front window and page through one of the dozens of papers on the counter. When you're bored with that, spend a few minutes reading the bathroom graffiti.

McShea's Restaurant & Bar. 242 Haverford Ave., Narberth. 610-667-0510. www.mcsheas.com. Bring a book or your laptop; free wifi.

Moriarty's. 1116 Walnut St., Center City east. 215-627-7676. www.moriartyspub.com. A quiet Irish pub seems like a contradiction in terms, but the mood here is as mellow as Dublin.

Quotations. 37 E. State St., Media. 610-627-2515. Wall-to-wall TVs and famous quotes make for a literary sports bar. The kind of place Bill Conlin would hang out in.

Westy's. 1440 Callowhill St., Spring Garden. 215-563-6134. Located right next door to the *Inquirer* and *Daily News*, at lunchtime it attracts editors reading today's rag or tomorrow's copy.

DRINK THIS

6 literary beers:

Anchor Steam. Jack London's drink of choice, in *John Barleycorn.*

Fred. A strong, hoppy ale from Portland's Hair of the Dog, inspired by Fred Eckhardt, the West Coast's ageless beer writer.

Gonzo Imperial Porter. A Baltic porter from Denver's Flying Dog, brewed in honor of Dr. Hunter S. Thompson, with label artwork by *Fear and Loathing in Las Vegas* artist Ralph Steadman.

Pliny the Elder. Russian River's massively hoppy ale is named after prolific ancient Roman scholar Gaius Plinius Secundus, who created the botanical name for hops, *lupus Salictarius,* meaning "wolf among scrubs."

Rogue Shakespeare Stout. "For a quart of ale is a dish for a king" (*The Winter's Tale*, IV, iii).

Thomas Hardy's Ale. Collect a library of vintages of this strong British ale that goes back to 1968, in honor of the author of all that boring Brit Lit you skipped in high school.

" When I read about the evils of drinking, I gave up reading. **"**

—Henny Youngman

BILL CONLIN'S TOP 6 BARROOM BRAWLS

4. Paul Owens vs. Irish Mike Ryan, multiple bouts

The Pope's [Owens's] favorite road drinking buddy was bullpen coach Mike Ryan. The affable New Englander held his liquor well and was a physical presence capable of keeping Owens from getting popped. Irish also had a stunt man's knack of slipping a punch and making it look like he had been hit with a haymaker. He and Owens would stage mock arguments, and they would always end the same way: Owens, the skinny and much older man, being browbeaten by the physically imposing younger man. It would end with Ryan pushing Owens or slapping him with an open hand. Owens would bellow, "That's it you son of a bitch," and launch a huge right hand. Ryan would go down like a pole-axed bull. The Pope would take a step back, shrug, and announce, "I warned him, but he didn't listen." At that point Mike would spring to his feet laughing and Owens would buy a round for the bar. They probably did it a dozen times in Sally's, the New York Sheraton bar where they knew all the bartenders and waitresses and had a transient crowd to shock with their choreographed "gotcha."

CHAPTER 8

Beer and Food

GOOD BEER GRUB

For those who are utterly convinced that it doesn't get any better than beer and pretzels, allow me to point you in the direction of **Twenty21**, the modern-looking bistro hidden at the base of one of those ugly office buildings on West Market Street in Center City.

This is a tony joint that was once known primarily for its 15-foot-high bar, a rather silly inconvenience that necessitated the occasionally exciting glimpse of barmaids climbing a ladder to fetch top-shelf whiskeys.

The ladder's still there, but these days the tastier treat can be found at floor level, in the form of a fresh glass of **Old Rasputin**, the Russian imperial stout from Northern California, and chocolate-covered espresso beans. We're talking huge reams of mouth-watering bittersweet arousal.

The beer-and-chocolate pairing is part of a well-conceived $20 appetizer plate that matches a flight of premium beers with a variety of finger foods. It's just the ticket for discovering, for example, how the aromatic wheat in **Bells Oberon Ale** is enhanced by a slice of fresh fig.

It's a long way from Old Milwaukee and Doritos.

EAT AND DRINK HERE

Because, as they say, good beer is good food.

Bridgid's. 726 N. 24th St., Fairmount. 215-232-3232. www.bridgids. com. Used to be everything on the bar menu was 5 bucks. Prices have crept upwards, but the food is still a value. (Duck confit for $8). Do yourself a favor; share a 750 ml **Moinette Belgian** ale, and eat at the horseshoe bar where the conversation welcomes you warmly into this cozy Fairmount neighborhood pub.

Byrne's Tavern. 3301 Richmond St., Port Richmond. 215-423-3444. OK, the beer selection needs a boost (Yuengling or Guinness is your best bet). But this Port Richmond joint, just off I-95, may have the best basic bar food in Philly. Platters of crabs, huge potato logs, meaty spiced wings, and, when available, the tastiest corn on the cob I've ever had in a restaurant.

The Farmhouse. 1449 Chestnut St., Emmaus. 610-967-6225. www.thefarmhouse.com. Even without the beer list this would be an excellent restaurant. Make it a one-two stop with your quarterly trek to Shangy's, the mammoth beer distributor right down the road. Or, drop in one night for a regularly scheduled beer dinner hosted by John Hansell, editor of the *Malt Advocate*, also published nearby.

Monk's Café. 264 S. 16th St., Center City west. 215-545-7005. www.monkscafe.com. The everyday menu pairs standard Belgian dishes (mussels cooked in ale) nicely. But to see chef Adam Glickman shine, you have to chow down at one of Monk's frequent beer dinners, usually focusing on a brewery or beer style and featuring exotic meats and fresh shellfish.

Standard Tap. 901 N. 2nd St., Northern Liberties. 215-238-0630. www.standardtap.com. *Bon Appetit* named the "gastropub" its 2006 restaurant trend of the year, and then declared that no place in the world embodies it better than Standard Tap. Hell, Philly locals have known it since this place began frying smelts and serving local drafts in 1999.

Tria Café. 123 S. 18th St., Center City west, 215-972-8742; 12th and Spruce sts., Washington Square West, 215.629.9200. www.triacafe.com. The cornerstone of these two small cafés is a trio of fermented food: beer, wine, and cheese. Can't speak for the wine, but the beer list is possibly the tidiest in the city: There's not a loser in the bunch. And the waitstaff knows exactly which tapas plates pair best with the suds. Try the stinky Italian Rebruschon and a bottle of smoky **Aecht Schlenkerla Rauchbier Urbock.**

ONE VERY, UM, UNUSUAL BEER-AND-FOOD JOINT

The Dive. 947 E. Passyunk Ave., South Philly. 215-465-5505. Here's a menu that comes straight from the frozen food aisle at the Acme to your plate. This joint's "plethora of gourmet offerings" includes fast dishes from all the great chefs: Chef Boyardee, Marie Callender, Mama Celeste, and, of course, the House of Stouffer. Like the owner says, when it's 1 a.m. and you've got the munchies, you really can't beat Hot Pockets.

EAT AND BYO HERE

Forget the wine—bring your beer to these top food joints instead:

Chloe. 232 Arch St., Old City. 215-629-2337. No reservations, so leave your cell number and hang out at **Charlie's Pub** (114 N. 3rd St.), just up the street.

Nearest takeout: Mulberry Market, 236 Arch St.

Dmitri's. 795 S. 3rd St., Queen Village. 215-625-0556. Greek. Wait for your table across the street at the **New Wave Café.**

Nearest takeout: New Wave Café, 784 S. 3rd St., or **For Pete's Sake**, 900 S. Front St.

Hamlet Bistro. 7105 Emlen St., West Mount Airy. 215-247-5800. Small, romantic room, Italian fare.

Nearest takeout: McMenamin's Tavern, 7170 Germantown Ave.

Il Cantuccio. 701 N. 3rd St. Northern Liberties. 215-627-6573. Classic Italian. I know, the temptation is to bring a bottle of Chianti, but try **Flying Fish Belgian Abbey Dubbel** with your risotto.

Nearest takeout: The Foodery, 837 N. 2nd St.

Matyson. 37 S. 19th St., Center City west. 215-564-2925. A tough reservation, but worth the wait.

Nearest takeout: Philly Nosheri Deli, 236 S. 21st St.

Trio. 2624 Brown St., Fairmount. 215-232-8746. Pan Asian cuisine.

Nearest takeout: Rose's Deli, 565 N. 20th St.

INSIDER TIP

The Greater Philadelphia Tourism Marketing Corporation has an online map of more than 200 BYOs in the city. Click on www.gophila.com/byobmap.

Though it's intended for winos, the search engine at www.dininginfo.com allows you to search for Philly area joints where you can bring your own beer.

YOUR OWN BOTTLE

Worried about looking unrefined when you pull out a sixpack at a fancy-schmancy BYO? Look for a large, corked 750 ml bottle from Stoudt's, Sly Fox, or Victory. It looks like wine and, guaranteed, it'll taste better than what they're drinking at the next table.

EAT AND DRINK THIS

Enjoy these great takeout flavors in your home with your own stash:

Celebrator Doppelbock and Sauerbraten from Rieker's. The creamy malt monster from Germany's Ayinger brewery is added gravy on this classic beef dish, served ready to eat from a Northeast Philly gem.

Riekers Prime Meats. 7979 Oxford Ave., Fox Chase. 215-745-3114.

Hennepin Ale and Chabis Feuille from DiBruno's. The effervescent saison cuts right through the creamy nuttiness of this French goat cheese. Excellent for a picnic.

DiBruno's. 930 S. 9th St., South Philly, 215-922-2876; 1730 Chestnut St., Rittenhouse Square, 215-665-9220.

Hitachino Nest White Ale and spring rolls from Vietnam Restaurant. Don't screw around with that weak Vietnamese 33 Export—hop over to Japan for the best witbier outside of Brussels. And make sure you get extra dipping sauce for those rolls.

Vietnam Restaurant. 221 N. 11th St., Chinatown. 215-592-1163.

Penn Dark and white pizza from Taconelli's. Usually, you'd go for a full-bodied lager with pizza, but Taconelli's is so big on the garlic, you want a roasty—but still very easy-drinking—beer for this meal.

Tacconelli's. 2604 E. Somerset St., Port Richmond. 215-425-4983.

Stoudt's Fat Dog Stoudt and Bassett's Mocha Chip ice cream float. Beer and ice cream? It sounds gross, but we're talking about either the sweetest stout or the roastiest ice cream you've ever tasted.

Bassett's available at **Whole Foods Market** or through www.bassetsicecream.com.

Victory Festbier and Roast Pork with Broccoli Rabe from Tony Luke's. The sports bar across the street will serve you this sandwich with a macro beer, but you're better off standing in line at the original and grabbing one to go. Then enjoy it with this almost smokey, full-flavored lager.

Tony Luke's. 39 E. Oregon Ave., South Philly. 215-551-5725.

UMM-UMM, GOOD

Wegmans market (1056 E. Lancaster Ave., Downingtown) serves soup made with Victory beer. Try the creamy HopDevil cheddar soup.

❝ No soldier can fight unless he is properly fed on beef and beer. **❞**

—John Churchhill,
First Duke of Marlborough

CHEESE AND BEER

You spend a few hours with drooling, 300-pound behemoths knocking heads, fighting for every inch of turf—it can get pretty nasty around the buffet table. Remember the hit Chuck Bednarik put on Frank Gifford back in 1960? Well, maybe not, but that was an afternoon tea party compared to the violence wrought in my den when the Buffalo wings run out during the Super Bowl.

It goes without saying that beer is the main course during Eagles games in my den.

And to accompany the suds?

Cheese. Stinky cheese.

I know what you're thinking. Joe Sixpack must've taken a hit from Brian Dawkins. Cheese? That's for Chablis-sippers at Old City art galleries.

Well, I've got one question for you doubters: What do you think they put on Doritos?

EAT AND DRINK THIS

Lip-smacking beer-and-cheese pairs:

Chimay Cinq Cents and Chimay cheese. Made by the same monastery that produces the beer, this is a funky medium-soft cheese that won't overwhelm the ale.

Prima Pils and Tilsiter Gourmant. A semifirm German table cheese, it's like Havarti, but less fatty. Victory's light, hoppy pilsener won't wipe out the cheese's flavor.

Saison Dupont and Pont-l'Eveque. From Normandy, this is a real stinker, thanks to its daily washings with brine. It might remind you of Camembert, only fuller—enough to stand up to the world's greatest saison-style ale, from Belgium.

Trois Pistoles and Oka. Make sure you get the raw-milk version of this monastery cheese from Canada; it stands up nicely to the strong, port-like flavor of the Three Pistols from Quebec.

Weyerbacher Heresy and Boerenkaas Gouda. Aged three to four years, this Netherlands farmhouse cheese is filled with crystallized fats that crunch to the bite. Wash them down with a rich, dark imperial stout from Easton.

Young's Old Nick and Colston Bassett Stilton. Stilton and barleywine go together like bangers and mash—it is the classic English pub snack. To step up the ale a notch, pull out that **J.W. Lees Vintage Harvest** you've got aging in the cellar.

BUY HERE

Top-of-the-line cheese shops:

Carlino's Specialty Foods. 2614 E. County Line Rd., Ardmore.
Chestnut Hill Cheese Shop. 8509 Germantown Ave., Chestnut Hill.
Claudio King of Cheese. 926 S. 9th St., Italian Market.
Cote & Co. 800 North Easton Rd., Doylestown.
DiBruno Brothers House of Cheese. 930 S. 9th St., Italian Market, and 1730 Chestnut St., Center City.
Downtown Cheese. Reading Terminal Market, 12th and Arch sts., Ardmore Farmer's Market, 200 Suburban Sq., Ardmore.

PHILLY FACT

DiBruno Bros. hosts frequent beer-and-cheese tastings at its Center City shop. For more info visit www.dibruno.com.

> **❝** Beer . . . can find such harmony with cheese that you won't know where the beer ends and the cheese begins. **❞**
>
> —Garrett Oliver,
> brewmaster, Brooklyn Brewing

MY FAVORITE BEER QUOTES

KWY Anchor **LARRY MENDTE** ► a Guinness fan names his favorite beer quotes:

"Why is American beer served cold? So you can tell it from urine."

—David Moulton

"Beer is living proof that God loves us and wants us to be happy."

—Benjamin Franklin

"You can't be a real country unless you have beer and an airline. It also helps if you have some kind of football team or some nuclear weapons. But, at the very least, you need a beer."

—Frank Zappa

"Not all chemicals are bad. Without chemicals such as hydrogen and oxygen, for example, there would be no way to make water, a vital ingredient in beer."

—Dave Barry

"I am a firm believer in the people. If given truth, they can be depended upon to meet any national crisis. The great point is to bring them the real facts, and beer."

—Abraham Lincoln

"All right brain, I don't like you and you don't like me, so just get me through this exam and I can go back to killing you slowly with beer."

—Homer Simpson

PHILLY FAVORITES

We're pessimistic, obnoxious, uncultured, disagreeable, and, besides that, we throw beer at the other team. And now, a word in defense of Philly attitude:

Cheesesteaks....

Only a place with so much edge and grime could create this greasy, gluttonous wonder.

In nicer cities, where the people are polite and smart, they eat salads ... and they are bored.

Cheesesteaks are not health food. They have no hint of anything green. They are red meat and yellow cheese and browned onions dripping with oil, and we laugh—laugh!—at the fat that fills our arteries.

Only a city with the self-confidence built upon 300 years of history could revel in such simplicity without pretension.

In newer cities, where the people are savvy and hip, they eat stylish, vertical food ... and they are hungry.

This is not fine dining. There aren't any stinkin' tablecloths. You wolf it down while standing up, preferably on a curb next to an idling Chevy.

A cheesesteak is in your face, just like the city's people. Hot and spicy, they confront you with their boldness. Unwieldy and sloppy, they challenge you to react.

EAT CHEESESTEAKS HERE

Most of the classics (Pat's, Geno's) don't have licenses, so BYO and be discreet. Otherwise, here are places that sell beer, wid...:

Abner's. 3813 Chestnut St., University City. 215-662-0100. Head over after the game at the Palestra.

Chubby's. 5826 Henry Ave., Roxborough. 215-487-2575. Possibly the only authentic cheesesteak shop that serves boilermakers.

Jim's Steaks. 400 South St., South Street. 215-928-1911. With its sizeable cooler, this is the best beer and cheesesteak combo in town.

McNally's Tavern. 8634 Germantown Ave., Chestnut Hill. 215-247-9736. Pass the cheesesteak and go straight for the famous Schmitter.

Philadelphia Steaks and Hoagies. 6410 S.E. Milwaukie Ave., Portland, Ore. 503-239-8544. OK, you've got to fly all the way to the Northwest for this one, but here's an out-of-town brewpub run by a Philly expatriate that specializes in our hometown favorites, including Tastykakes.

Tony's Luke's Beef & Beer. 26 E. Oregon Ave., South Philly. 215-551-5725. Beer's only OK, but the roast pork and greens are why you're here. Across street from original Tony Luke's stand.

EAT PIZZA HERE

These joints serve beer with pies:

Best House Pizzeria. 4301 Baltimore Ave., University City. 215-386-1450. A University City hangout attracting profs and anarchists. Pizza's only OK, but the beer's worth the stop.

Mama Palma's. 2229 Spruce St., Fitler Square. 215-735-7357. This joint gets it right on both the pizza and the beer. Crispy wood–fired–oven crusts, excellent crafts, and Belgians.

Ortino's Pizzeria. 800 Main St., Schwenksville. 610-287-8333. www.ortinos.com. A huge surprise on the main drag in a dusty, old town along the Perkiomen. Four primo taps (**Sly Fox** is always on) with craft and Belgian bottles. A nice pit stop for cyclists along the trail to Green Lane.

Pietro's Coal Oven Pizzeria. 1714 Walnut St., Center City. 215-735-8090. www.pietrospizza.com. Very good pizzas, or save the calories and go for a mammoth salad. Either way, a very nice tap list and **Orval** in bottles.

Tony's Place. 6300 Frankford Ave., Mayfair. 215-535-9851. The classic Philadelphia tomato pie, and with a bit of luck you'll find **Smithwick's** on tap or **Flying Fish** in bottles. Down the block is **The Grey Lodge Pub**, which also serves tomato pie.

Tony's Place Bar and Grill. 1297 Greeley Ave., Ivyland. 215-675-7275. Same family as above, so you know you're going to get a good pie. Better beer here, though, with 10 drafts, including **Sam Adams, Franziskaner, Flying Fish, Victory,** and **Sierra Nevada.**

EAT THESE MUNCHIES

Pair these local favorites with a local brew:

Fisher's Soft Pretzel and Victory St. Boisterous. A doppelbock and a doughy pretzel from the Reading Terminal Market? Consider it the anti-Atkins diet.

Habbersett Scrapple and Stoudt's Weizen. A pairing of two Pennsylvania Dutch favorites (and, don't laugh, in Bavaria, wheat beer is known as breakfast beer).

Pop's Water Ice and Yards Saison. Order a large lemon, suck half of it down, then pour in the beer. Instant brain freeze!

Primo's Italian Hoagie and Sly Fox Phoenix Pale Ale. You're going to want some hops to cut through all that prosciutto. You're going to want a can, not a bottle, to slide right inside that thin paper bag.

Tastykake Butterscotch Krimpets and Flying Fish Hopfish India Pale Ale. Second to only Frank's Black Cherry Wishniak and Peanut Butter Kandy Kakes as the ideal lunchbag dessert.

Utz Salt & Malt Vinegar Potato Chips and Stegmaier 1857 Lager. You'll need two bottles of this nicely sweetened lager to balance one bag of these tart, lip-smacking chips.

❝ Without question, the greatest invention in the history of mankind is beer. Oh, I grant you that the wheel was also a fine invention, but the wheel does not go nearly as well with pizza. **❞**

—Dave Barry

BILL CONLIN'S TOP 6 BARROOM BRAWLS

5. Paul Owens vs. Phillies Minor League Director Jim Baumer, 1983

On the eve of the '83 League Championship Series against the Dodgers in Los Angeles, Owens, then the manager, threw punches at Baumer in two different bars in the Wilshire Hyatt Hotel. When Owens was asked to replace fired manager Pat Corrales (with the Phils tied for first place) that July, he suspected (correctly) that Phils president Bill Giles was hoping he would fail so he could take over the GM function himself (which he did anyway). But Owens surprised a lot of people by rallying the "Wheeze Kids" to an amazing September and an easy division title. Owens hated Baumer, whom he accused of sniping behind his back and laughing at his "managing" style. (Bobby Wine made most of the tough in-game decisions.) When Baumer and several scouts walked into the hotel bar after the club came back from a Dodger Stadium workout, he ran into an Owens with blood in his eye. Baumer was younger and stronger than Owens, but he was a wimp. Owens nailed him with two or three good shots (I was told) before it was broken up. Both men went to their rooms to shower and dress for dinner. Owens met Mike Ryan and several of his coaches in a cocktail bar on the mezzanine level. The Pope's [Owens's] 1980 World Series ring glinted noticeably. Baumer and his entourage swept in and it was on again almost immediately. I witnessed Round 2. Before it was broken up, Owens opened a cut on Baumer's cheekbone with his ring.

CHAPTER 9

Going Home

DISTRIBUTORS

Your average beer distributor looks like something out of the last scene of *Raiders of the Lost Ark*. Housed in a tin Quonset hut, it's dimly lit and dirty. Stacks of dust-covered cases sit on splintered pallets, grouchy clerks crouch behind bulletproof cashier windows, age-old bottles from an extinct brewery await a clueless buyer. There's no price list. The place's idea of merchandising is Miss Michelob's semi-annual T-shirt giveaway.

Admittedly, the whole seedy atmosphere has its appeal. Hunting for your favorite brew without the assault of slick advertising is a refreshing break from those obsequious money-grubbers at McDonald's and Banana Republic.

And, what the hell, beer basically sells itself, right?

6 ESSENTIALS

Huge case selection and excellent beer knowledge give these joints the edge:

The Beer Yard. 218 E. Lancaster Ave., Wayne. 610-688-3431.
www.beeryard.com. Cramped quarters, but the owners always know exactly where your favorite box is buried. Its informative web site is a beer freak's go-to resource: www.beeryard.com.

Bell Beverage. 2809 S. Front St., South Philly. 215–468–0222. www.bellbeverage.com. Discount prices on many craft beers, easy access right off the I-95 Front Street exit.

Hatboro Beverage. 201 Jacksonville Rd., Hatboro. 215-675-1078. www.hatbev.com. Frequent beer tastings with area breweries.

Kunda Beverage. 349 S. Henderson Rd., King of Prussia. 610-265-3113. www.kundabev.com. Thanks to a recent licensing rights shuffle, it now handles dozens of new out-of-state micros and imports. Good beer list at www.kundabev.com.

Shangy's—The Beer Authority. 40 E. Main St., Emmaus. 610-967-1701. Well over 2,500 different labels, specializing in unusual European and out-of-state microbrews.

Stone's Beverage Center. 1701 Fairmount Ave., Fairmount. www.stonesbeverage.com. The closest, best beer selection to Center City, specializing in locals.

OTHER RECOMMENDED DISTRIBUTORS

▶ CITY

The Beer Outlet. 77 Franklin Mills Blvd., Franklin Mills. 215-632-5035.

Brewers Outlet. 7401 Germantown Pike, W. Mount Airy. 215-247-1265.

Doc's World of Beer. 701 E. Cathedral Rd. (Andorra Shopping Center), Roxborough. 215-482-4338.

Nicoletti Beverage Center. 7040 State Rd., Tacony. 215-624-3184.

Society Hill Beverage. 129 Washington Ave., Queen Village. 215-336-7622.

The Beer Guys. 1305 West Chester Pike, Havertown. 610-688-3431.

Bound Beverage. 2544 Bristol Pike, Bensalem. 215-639-0635.

Edgemont Beer & Cigars. 5042B West Chester Pike, Newtown
Square. 610-353-8848.

Exton Beverage Center. 310 E. Lincoln Highway, Exton.
610-363-7020.

Manoa Beverage. 1111 West Chester Pike, Havertown. 610-446-1111.

Stockertown Beverage Center. 515 Main St., Stockertown.
610-746-5611.

Tanczos Beverages. 2330 Jacksonville Rd., Bethlehem.
610-866-8039.

❝ 24 hours in a day, 24 beers in a case.
Coincidence? I think not. ❞

—Attributed to numerous comedians

SIXPACK TO GO

Logic would tell you the best place for a broad selection should be distributors. But Pennsylvania's anticonsumer liquor law defies logic and
forbids them from selling anything less than a case.

That minimum isn't such a big deal when you're talking about laying out 15 bucks for a mainstream beer you've tasted 100 times before. Sooner or later, you're going to finish off all 24 bottles.

Micros and imports are a different matter, though. At 30 bucks or more a case, it's like putting all your chips on double-zero and hoping you'll like the taste of that chocolate-raspberry porter.

So what do you do if you want just six bottles of a potentially great beer? Well, it's back to those takeouts. Thankfully, a handful in the city and 'burbs provide an extraordinary selection.

BUY HERE

CITY

Avoid joints with bulletproof glass:

The Foodery. 324 S. 10th St., Washington Square West, 215-928-1111; 837 N. 2nd St., Northern Liberties, 215-238-6077. www.fooderybeer.com. By far, the best takeout beer store in the region, with more Belgians, Germans, Brits, American micros, and even vintage ales than anyone else. Very knowledgeable staff. Tight quarters and tough parking at the Center City location make the newer, more spacious Northern Liberties spot (across from **Standard Tap**) the new go-to choice.

Kitchen USA. 1933 Spruce St., Center City west. 215–545–1722. Not a huge selection, but some surprises and cigars.

Latimer Deli. 255 S. 15th St., Center City west. 215-545-9244. A very surprising selection that's invaluable when you forget to bring a bottle to one of Center City's trendy BYO's. Many large bottles.

Philly Nosheri Deli. 236 S. 21st St., Center City west. 215-567-3392.

Rose's Deli. 565 N. 20th St., Fairmount. 215-563-2328. Coolers behind the counter inhibit browsing, but the selection is very neat in this neighborhood spot.

The Six Pack Store. 7015 Roosevelt Blvd., Northeast. 215-338-6384. Too much space given over to macros, but it's still Northeast Philly's best takeout. Get in the local lanes northbound on the Boulevard; just beyond Levick Street, it's on your right at Tyson Avenue.

Spruce Market. 1523 Spruce St., Center City west. 215–735–3382.

'BURBS

Excellent delis hit the mark:

Boccella's Deli. 37 W. Eagle Rd., Havertown. 610-789-2228.

Candlewyck Lounge. 2551 Durham Rd., Buckingham. 215-794-8233. Near the crossroads of routes. 413, 263, and 202 in Buxco. Anything you find in the large bank of coolers can be taken over to the adjoining bar for immediate consumption.

Capone's. 22 W. Germantown Pike, Norristown. 610-279-4748. Tidy back room, with some unusual brands, behind a full-service bar that is quickly building a rep for rare micros and special events.

Epicurean Restaurant and Bar. 902 Village at Eland, Rt. 113, Phoenixville. 610-933-1336. www.americabarandgrill.com. The fine restaurant has an adjoining takeout shop featuring many beers. Gift baskets can be ordered (but they're pricey).

Landis Restaurant. 118 W. Lancaster Ave., Wayne. 610-688-5895. More than 150 beers, plus cigars.

Mesquito Grille. 128 W. State St., Doylestown. 215-230-7427. Everything on the beer menu, including draft beer, is available to go.

Michael's Deli. 130 Town Center Rd., Valley Forge Shopping Center, King of Prussia. 610-265-3265. www.michaelsdeli.com. All the locals plus decent imports. Grab a bottle and a hoagie.

Ron's School House Grille. 74 E. Uwchlan Ave., Exton. 610-594-9900.

Trenton Road Takeout. 1024 Trenton Rd., Fallsington. 215-736-1389. Probably the best in the suburbs with a 500-plus beer list. Look for gift packs and 5-liter cans.

NEW JERSEY

Big wine outlets make room for brew:

Joe Canal's Discount Liquor Mart. www.joecanals.com. Big, warehouse-style markets that have been steadily improving their high-end beer. Look for the chain in Hammonton, Lawrenceville, Hamilton, Marlton, Delran, Millville, Williamstown, and Egg Harbor Township.

Martin's Liquors. 3601 Rt. 38 (at Marter Ave.), Mt. Laurel. 856-235-2273.

Monster Beverage. 1299 N. Delsea Dr., Glassboro. 856-881-2580. If you can't make it to the Foodery, shop here. The selection is almost as big and the prices are better. Buy everything from single bottles to full cases.

Red White and Brew. 33 High St., Mount Holly. 609-702-9949. www.redwhiteandbrew.net. A nicely organized bottle shop with good service. Especially good on North Jersey beers (**Ramstein**) that rarely make it below Princeton. Word is they'll be expanding to the shore.

Total Wine. 2100 Rt. 38 (at Cherry Hill Mall), Cherry Hill.
856-667-7101.

Walker's Wine & Spirits. 86 Bridge St., Lambertville.
609-397-0625.

Wegman's. 240 Nassau Park Blvd., Princeton. 609-919-9300.
A grocery store with beer, how about that? Prices are steep, but
you can stock up for an entire party in one stop.

DELAWARE AND MARYLAND

Look for oddball out-of-staters that you can't find in the city:

F&N Wine & Spirits. 2094 Naamans Rd., Wilmington, Del.
302-475-4496.

Kreston Wine & Spirits. 904 Concord Ave., Wilmington, Del.
302-652-3792.

Total Wine. 691 Naamans Rd., Claymont, Del., 302-792-1322; 1325
McKennans Church Rd., Wilmington, Del., 302-994-5510.

State Line Liquors. 1610 Elkton Road, Elkton, Md. 800-446-9463.
www.statelineliquors.com. Get off I-95 at the Elkton exit, just
below the first toll. Excellent micros and Belgians, single bottles,
tastings. One of the best value shops in the region.

BEER–TO–GO RULES

Buying a beer to take home is still an ordeal in the Quaker state.
Here's the rundown of rules:

PENNSYLVANIA

Retail distributors
Sell beer by the case, keg.
Open 7 days a week (Sundays noon–5 p.m.).

Taverns
Beer by the sixpack or single.
Two-sixpack maximum per sale. Multiple sales permitted.
Most open 7 days a week, till 2 a.m.

Takeout shops
Rules same as taverns. Hours vary.

Wine and spirits
Available to go only at state-owned liquor stores.

NEW JERSEY AND DELAWARE

All alcohol sold in liquor stores, open 7 days a week. Some supermarket sales. No sales in convenience stores.

TRAVEL ADVISORY

For years, Pennsylvania State Police monitored the border for out-of-state beer shoppers bringing back discount cases from Jersey and Delaware. But word is the cops have better things to do. Just keep an eye out for Crown Vics tailing you out of the parking lots on Camden's Admiral Wilson Boulevard.

HOMEBREW

Saturday morning around my place frequently is accompanied by the sweet smell of malt and cigar smoke. But this isn't the morning after a Friday-night poker game. It's Joe Sixpack's Rowhouse Brewery.

With a few big pots and inexpensive ingredients, I cook up some of the meanest ales you'll ever taste.

Now, that's no invitation for you freeloaders to show up on my front stoop with a mug in your hand. You mooches can go make your own beer—it's about as easy as barbecuing on a Weber grill, and it'll cost you under 20 bucks a case.

6 ESSENTIALS

These shops will get you started on a Philly brew of your own:

Barry's Homebrew Outlet. 101 Snyder Ave., South Philly. 215-755-4556.

Beercrafters Inc. 110A Greentree Rd., Turnersville, N.J. 856-227-9348.

Brew Your Own Beer. 2026 Darby Rd., Havertown. 610-449-5496.

Home Sweet Homebrew. 2008 Sansom St., Center City west. 215-569-9469.

Keystone Homebrew Supply. 779 Bethlehem Pike, Montgomeryville. 215-885-0100.

Wine, Barley & Hops. 248 Bustleton Pike, Feasterville. 215-322-4780.

> **❝** Give a man a beer and he'll waste an hour. Teach a man to brew beer and he'll waste a lifetime. **❞**
>
> —Unknown

INSIDER TIP

Want to hone your skills? Contact a brewery and volunteer to help. Often, breweries need extra hands on the bottling line.

HOME BAR

A man's bar, I think we can all agree, is the very essence of his being. It is the place where he feels most comfortable, where he can be moody or happy or just tie one on without excuse.

It is sanctuary, yes, but it's also an expression of character. Like the beer I drink, my bar would be handcrafted, bold, and rich with flavor. It would be as warm as a mouthful of whiskey tickling the throat. Visitors would be awed by its subtle undertones. When they carry me out, I want the paramedics to say, "Yo, nice bar."

6 ESSENTIALS

It takes more than beer to fill up your home bar:

Bar stools. Where else, but Mr. Bar Stool? This is a classic Philly resource with hundreds of styles. 167 N. 2nd St., Old City. 215-925-4800.

Beer fridge. Look for an inexpensive wine fridge, then replace the curved shelves with flat racks, to stand up those bottles. Racks available at Grand Restaurant Equipment Co., 1025 Cherry St., Chinatown. 215-928-0880.

Gadgets. Beer taps, hose, fittings, CO_2 regulators—get them where the pros shop, at Springfield Beer Parts, 600 Schuylkill Ave., near South Street Bridge. 215-546-5051.

Kegs. Instead of committing your Beer Meister to an entire quarter keg, stock it with two smaller one-sixth kegs, called sixtels. They're now available at most distributors, including Exton Beverage Center (310 E. Lincoln Highway, Exton), with a very healthy supply. Gen. Lafayette Inn & Brewery (646 Germantown Pike, Lafayette Hill) sells 5-gallon minikegs filled with its brews for just $49.

Memorabilia. Ebay's good for old Philly gear (Esslinger, Gretz, Ortlieb's, and Schmidt's). Eastern Coast Breweriana Association holds annual shows at the Valley Forge Convention Center. Members receive *The Keg*, a quarterly magazine about old breweries and collectibles. www.eastcoastbrew.com.

Neon signs. If you left that old one in your college dorm, check out the supply at The Cellar, 87 S. Main St., New Hope. 215-534-1586. More supplies at The Pub Shoppe, 978 Lindsay Ln., Lancaster. 888-384-3782. www.thepubshoppe.com.

---

6 ESSENTIAL GLASSES

Get more enjoyment when you drink out of the proper glass:

British pint. Not those dingy 16-ouncers, but 20 ounces (with a small bulge for gripping) to handle a proper pint.

Dimple mug. Keeps your warm hand off the cold lager, and it's heavy enough to clink glasses (without bashing your fingers).

Goblet. The ideal glass for admiring the color and character of your ale. Its heavy base balances the glass nicely in your hand.

Pilsener. Tall and thin, it shows off the golden color and allows the CO_2 to bubble nicely into a foamy head.

Tulip or thistle. Shaped like a tulip petal, it's designed to capture the foam while allowing you to stick your nose right into the aromatic pillow.

Weizen. Tall enough to handle a pint of gushing wheat beer, thick enough to keep it cool.

“ Your first sip is with your eyes. ”

—Anonymous beer judge

GET A COMPLETE SET

The essential beer glass set includes 6 must-have glasses for beer-drinking pleasure, including a hard-to-find Imperial pint (23 oz.), for $37 plus shipping. Available from Beerheads.com (a Philly company). 800-832-2436.

6 ESSENTIAL SOURCES

Where to buy, not steal, your own mug:

Any brewpub or brewery. Nearly all of them sell something with their logo, usually 5 bucks or less per pint.

Home Sweet Homebrew. Ignore the cat, climb over the sacks of grain, and check out the selection in the back. Take a whiff of hops—it might inspire you to homebrew. 2008 Sansom St., Center City west. 215-569-9469.

Make your own. Get beer glasses with your own name on them at www.pubglasses.com.

Online. Try BelgianExperts.com for beautiful glassware with Belgian logos.

Shangy's. Excellent selection, including unusual styles from European breweries. 40 E. Main St., Emmaus. 610-967-1701.

State Line Liquors. Wander back to the wine-tasting room to shelves of tulips, flutes, goblets, and more. 1610 Elkton Rd., Elkton, Md. 800-446-9463.

HEFE HELP

Take that German hefeweizen and invert the bottle completely inside the weizen glass. Then slowly pull the bottle upwards, releasing a steady stream of suds till the glass fills. Then roll the bottle lightly on a table to loosen the remaining yeast and foam and pour that into the glass, too.

INSIDER TIP

Don't use dish soap when washing your glassware. It kills the foam. Instead, either run them through the dishwasher or use a low-sudsing cleaner, like Beer Clean.

BILL CONLIN'S TOP 6 BARROOM BRAWLS

6. Paul Owens vs. Jane Doe, early '90s

The Pope [Owens] and his closest friends had a tendency to argue. His inner circle included Dallas Green, Hugh Alexander, and Ray Shore. One of their favorite locations for argument was Mike Houllis's Island House, a Greek restaurant in Clearwater Beach across from Heilman's Beachcomber. One night, Owens and Alexander got into a violent shouting match, featuring multiple "F" bombs. It became so heated that an elderly gentleman and his wife who were seated at a nearby table registered their displeasure. "Mind your own fucking business," Owens instructed. The old gentleman rose gallantly, followed by his wife. Owens got up, as did Alexander, who placed a restraining hand (his only hand) on the Pope's right shoulder. Owens threw a punch at Uncle Hughie. Uncle Hughie ducked. The frail woman had just stepped between Owens, Alexander, and her husband. The punch intended for Alexander caught the woman on the button. She went out like a light. Fortunately, she fell into her outraged husband's arms. While the Island House staff revived the wife, her husband was calling the police. A convoy of prowlers arrived. By that time, Houllis, Green, and Alexander had hidden Owens in a food storage area in the back of the restaurant. The police were there almost two hours, taking statements, interviewing witnesses. The man was not a baseball fan and had no idea who Owens was. No criminal charges were filed. But the husband was told by one of the witnesses that his wife had been popped by "That fellow who has something to do with the Phillies." The guy filed a big-ticket civil suit against Owens. [Phils president Bill] Giles said, "You're on your own on this one. Our lawyers won't touch it."

❝ He that drinketh strong beer and goes to bed right mellow, lives as he ought to live and dies a hearty fellow. **❞**

—Anonymous

NIGHTCAPS

At 2 a.m., closing time, the taps turn off. You down the last glass of whiskey, suck on the ice cubes, and head into the dark emptiness of a town that is suddenly, awfully bone dry.

Quaint, isn't it, that in a nonstop civilization, a man can't find a drink for a few hours every night.

Normally, you'd be tempted to chalk up such a cruel quirk to our uptight founders, the Quakers. Never completely comfortable with the notion that an adult might actually enjoy an occasional sensory numbing, our forefathers devoted themselves to the proposition that thou shall not be permitted to purchase more than two sixpacks in a tavern.

Last call, then, is a bit of government-mandated Quaker-style self-denial, a pause to reflect (or pass out).

DRINK THIS

Pull on your slippers and crack open one of these warming beers by the fireplace:

Dogfish Head Worldwide Stout. At about 20 percent alcohol, a single bottle is the equivalent of an entire sixpack of Guinness. Share it with someone; it's enough to put both of you into the proper mood before heading to the sack.

Iron Hill Russian Imperial Stout. One of the local brewpub chain's most honored beers is available in big, corked bottles. The roasty malt is so well balanced with American hops, the alcohol (8.3 percent) is almost a second thought.

Old Rasputin. This dark, bitter Russian imperial stout from California is just the thing to send you dreaming of the hereafter.

Slaapmutske. Taken from the Dutch word for nightcap, any of the three varieties from the De Smet brewery will do the trick, especially **Triple Nightcap**, an 8 percent golden ale.

Victory Old Horizontal. Flat out and feet first is exactly where you'll be headed after a bottle of this mellow barleywine. Sweet dreams.

Weyerbacher Hedonism. A dark ale with about 12 percent alcohol that will have you breaking out your crystal brandy snifter. Just don't drop it when you finish off the bottle.

> **"** Now it's closing time, the music's fading out. Last call for drinks, I'll have another stout. **"**
>
> —Tom Waits, *Closing Time*

HANGOVERS

Lucky for you, lately I've been drinking a lot more than usual.

It's all in the name of science, of course, as I conduct a groundbreaking road test of the new wave of antihangover pills, with names like The Chaser and RU-21.

Yes, I know, there's some risk, gobbling down these little pills. Who knows what's inside 'em?

But they must be safe. Surely, no one would make false advertising claims in the e-mail spam that fills my in-box. Especially when it comes from such internationally respected pharmaceutical companies as Lifestyle Marketing, Inc.

6 QUESTIONS

With little available scientific research, beer drinkers are left with folk remedies...and lots of headaches.

What causes a hangover? Alcohol is a diuretic, so, generally, it's dehydration. Lately, researchers have theorized the real pain may be the body's reaction to toxic byproducts of fermentation known as congeners.

Does it matter what you drink? It depends more on how much you drink. But the congener theory suggests that dark liquor is worse than clear. No clear data on the type of beer, however.

Can hangovers be prevented? Aside from knowing your own capacity, one trick that works is drinking water in between beers. The extra water hydrates your body and helps reduce total alcohol consumption.

What's in those hangover pills? Mostly vitamin supplements. Perfect Equation contains prickly pear cactus extract. The Chaser contains calcium carbonate and activated charcoal.

Do they work? Depends on whom you ask. But if you're looking for independent scientific analysis, forget it. None of the pills have undergone any peer review.

How about home remedies? There's been even less study about the effects of vitamin C, tomato juice, raw eggs, and hair of the dog. Personally speaking, a cheesesteak from Chubby's used to do the trick for me.

GETTING AROUND

If possible, walk—don't drive—especially in Center City. Parking is a hassle, and you'll find you can stroll 10 to 15 blocks in the time it would take to find a new space.

Plus, walking lets you see the city at its best—at sidewalk level. It's here where you'll notice that neon sign for a beer you never tasted, where you'll hear the sound of a jukebox blasting your favorite song.

Be curious; don't be afraid of a strange place. Taverns want your business and they will welcome you inside. Likewise, if it doesn't feel right, if it looks like they don't have a decent beer, leave. There's another joint just down the street.

AIR

Philadelphia International Airport is located in the southernmost section of the city. Cab rides cost $25 to Center City and take about 20 minutes, depending on traffic. The SEPTA R1 train, which runs every 30 minutes, is cheaper and takes you to 30th Street Station.

Airport: 800-PHL-GATE. www.phl.org.

Nearest beer: Independence Brew Pub between Terminals B and C. It's not really a brewpub, but it serves a good variety of locals. Look also for the multitap **Jet Rock Bar & Grill** in several of the terminals, serving mainstream with a local or two.

TRAINS

30th Street Station is the hub of all Amtrak and other trains into Philadelphia. It's located at 30th and Market in West Philly, just across the Schuylkill from Center City. It connects with SEPTA buses and the Frankford El, both of which provide quick access to Center City.

Amtrak: 215-349-2270. www.30thstreetstation.com.

Nearest beer: Bridgewater's Pub along the western side of 30th Street Station features a very good selection of micros.

Suburban Station, 16th Street and JFK Boulevard, is part of the hub for regional trains, from the suburbs and beyond—along with the stations at 30th Street and Market East (12th and Market). It's within walking distance of many fine bars and a short cab ride to hotels.

SEPTA trains: 215–580–7800.

Nearest beer: Tir na Nog Irish Bar & Grill, 1600 Arch St. (one block north of JFK). 215-514-1700. www.tirnanogphilly.com.

Bonus brew: If you're thirsty on the R7 to Trenton, hop off at the Torresdale Station, cross James Street, and duck into the **Three Monkeys Café.** 9645 James St. 215-637-6665. www.3monkeyscafe.com. Above–average blackboard menu with a handful of decent taps, including **Stoudt's.**

BUSES (OUT OF TOWN)

Greyhound and **Peter Pan** operate out of the Greyhound terminal at 10th and Filbert streets, Chinatown (just north of the Gallery mall).

Greyhound: 800-229-9424. www.greyhound.com.

Peter Pan: 800-343-9999. www.peterpanbus.com.

Nearest beer: SoleFood, lobby of Loew's Hotel, 1200 Market St. 215-627-1200. Skip right past the average taps at Champ's at the Marriot and camp out in this laid-back lounge with a full array of **Stoudt's.**

MASS TRANSIT

SEPTA, the regional transit authority, is bashed by locals, but it does provide excellent access to every part of the city via buses, trolleys, and subway. Fare is $2 per trip, $6 per day pass. Tokens cost $1.30 (minimum two) and are available in subway vending machines. Warning: some lines shut down at 1 a.m. 215-580-7800. www.septa.com (look for maps and schedules).

New Jersey Transit also provides buses into Center City. 215-569-3752. www.njtransit.com.

Nearest beer: There's probably a swig left in that brown paper bag on the back seat.

PHLASH

Those ugly purple "trolleys" you see creeping up Market Street are a cheap ride around Center City. Fares are $1 (all-day pass $4). They stop at 20 key locations between Penn's Landing and the Philadelphia Museum of Art, operating only from mid–May through Labor Day. www.phillyphlash.com.

Nearest beer: Get off at 2nd and Market and hit one of the joints listed in the Old City section (pp. 23–24).

CARS

Like any big city, traffic is heavy, especially during rush hour. Surprisingly, though, it can be decidedly light throughout Center City, because many people live within blocks of their workplaces.

It's parking that's the hassle. The city's Parking Authority is one of the most deviously efficient government units in the world. They will ticket you and ticket you hard. Fines start at $25, payable by mail, phone, or online.

Read the signs carefully. Parking in many spots is illegal during rush hour. Other spots are dedicated to handicapped drivers or valet services. Cars are towed to out-of-the-way lots operated by bureaucrats with the pleasant dispositions of caged pit bulls.

Private lots are expensive, up to $24 for a full day. At night, the going rate is $10 to $12.

Info on violations and parking lots: www.philapark.org.

TAXIS

You can flag down a taxicab on any street corner in Center City. For a guaranteed ride, head to a major hotel.

An average ride in Center City is between $7 and $10 plus tip.

Taxi service outside of Center City is much less certain. If you get a ride to a bar in the outskirts, get the driver's cell phone number and make arrangements to have him pick you up later. Otherwise, use one of these numbers and expect a minimum 15-minute wait:

City Cab. 215-492-6500.
Convention Cab. 215-462-0200.
Northeast Yellow Cab. 215-829-4222.
Olde City Taxi. 215-338-0838.
Quaker City. 215-728-8000.

DWI RULES

Point-zero-eight is now the rule of the land, like it or not. Exceed it anywhere near Philly, and you'll pay big bucks, even if it's your first offense.

PENNSYLVANIA

Penalties depend on blood alcohol percentage:

- **.08–.099**: $300 fine, 6 months maximum probation, attend driving school.
- **.10–.159**: 48 hours jail, $500–$5000 fine, 12-month license suspension, optional ignition lock, alcohol school.
- **Over .16**: 72 hours jail, $1,000–$5,000 fine, 12-month license suspension, alcohol school, drug and alcohol treatment, optional ignition lock.

NEW JERSEY

You can lose your car, in addition to huge fines:

- **$250–$400 fine,** plus court costs and fees of $355.
- **12–48 hours** in alcohol school.
- **30 days** maximum jail sentence.
- **$3000** in motor vehicle surcharges.
- **Insurance surcharges.**
- **Optional ignition lock.**

DELAWARE

Police confiscate your license upon arrest and issue a 15-day temp license. No new license until conviction is cleared.

- **Fines up to $1,150.**
- **Imprisonment up to 6 months.**
- **Optional ignition lock.**
- **DUI education course.**

HOW DRUNK ARE YOU (LOW-TECH)?

Here's a handy formula you can remember, even after a couple of rounds:

For each standard drink (one cocktail, one pint of beer, or one glass of wine), count 3 points. For each hour that you've been drinking, count 2 points. Add up your drink points and subtract your hour points.

If the result is less than 6, you should be OK to drive.

HOW DRUNK ARE YOU (HIGH-TECH)?

Some taverns are now installing coin-operated breathalyzers that are guaranteed to be accurate within .01 percent. Even better, buy your own handheld unit. You can find them for as little as $60 online, including at www.breathalcolyzer.com.

CHAPTER 10

Great American Beer Festival

It's the world's single-largest drinking event this side of Munich's Oktoberfest: 450-plus breweries, 1,800 beers, and more than 30,000 extremely serious, all-business, nose-to-the-grindstone conventioneers in downtown Denver.

We're talking three days of extensive, self-sacrificing research, if you know what I mean.

And for what?

For most of us, it's to hone our beer-consumption skills.

But for brewers, it's for the glory, and maybe prosperity. A GABF medal means you have arrived.

PHILADELPHIA MEDALISTS

Year	Brewery	Beer
2006	Bethlehem Brew Works	Berliner Weiss
2007	Bethlehem Brew Works	English-style IPA
1986	Dock Street	Dock Street
1992	Dock Street	Dock Street Cream Ale
2004	Dogfish Head	Midas Touch
2005	Dogfish Head	Midas Touch
2006	Dogfish Head	World Wide Stout
2006	Dogfish Head	Festina Lente
2007	Dogfish Head	Midas Touch
2000	General Lafayette	Alt! Who Goes There?
1996	Independence*	Independence Gold
1996	Independence*	Franklinfest
1998	Independence*	Franklinfest
1997	Iron Hill	Lodestone Lager
1998	Iron Hill	Wee Heavy
1999	Iron Hill Newark	Maibock
1999	Iron Hill West Chester	Vienna
2000	Iron Hill Media	Lodestone Lager
2000	Iron Hill Newark	Maibock
2001	Iron Hill Media	Wee Heavy
2002	Iron Hill Media	Pig Iron Porter
2002	Iron Hill West Chester	Tripel
2003	Iron Hill Media	Lambic de Hill
2003	Iron Hill Media	Tripel

Style	Medal
German-style wheat ale	Bronze
Pro-Am	Gold
Amber Ale	Consumer Preference
American cream ale/lager	silver
Specialty honey lager/ale	Gold
Specialty honey lager/ale	Silver
Aged beer	Bronze
Belgian-style sour ale	Bronze
Specialty honey lager/ale	Silver
German brown ale	Silver
Golden/Canadian ale	Bronze
Marzen/Oktoberfest	Gold
Marzen/Oktoberfest	Bronze
Munchener helles	Gold
Strong Scotch ale	Bronze
Bock	Gold
Vienna lager	Bronze
Munchener helles	Bronze
Bock	Bronze
Strong Scotch ale	Bronze
Robust porter	Bronze
Belgian abbey ale	Bronze
Belgian sour ale	Gold
Belgian abbey ale	Bronze

*Defunct

PHILADELPHIA MEDALISTS

Year	Brewery	Beer
2003	Iron Hill Newark	Russian Imperial Stout
2003	Iron Hill West Chester	Dunkel
2004	Iron Hill Wilmington	Bourbon Russian
2004	Iron Hill Wilmington	Tripel
2005	Iron Hill Newark	Ironbound Ale
2005	Iron Hill Wilmington	Belgian Strong
2005	Iron Hill Wilmington	Kriek de Hill
2006	Iron Hill Media	Russian Imperial Stout
2006	Iron Hill West Chester	Bourbon Ivan
2007	Iron Hill Media	Kriek de Hill
1999	John Harvard Wayne	Georgia Smoke
2001	John Harvard Wayne	Springfield Schwarz
2002	John Harvard Springfield*	Springfield Schwarz
2005	John Harvard Wayne	Devon Altbier
1994	Lion	Liebotschaner Cream
1994	Lion	1857
1995	Lion	Liebotschaner Cream
1999	Lion	Liebotschaner Cream
1999	Lion	Pocono Pilsner
2003	Lion	Stegmaier Gold Medal
2003	McKenzie Glen Mills	Trappist Pale Ale
2003	McKenzie Glen Mills	Saison
2004	McKenzie Glen Mills	Bavay
2006	McKenzie Glen Mills	Raven
2007	McKenzie	Saison Vautour
2007	McKenzie	Wee Heavy

Joe Sixpack's Philly Beer Guide

Style	Medal
Imperial stout	Gold
Munchner dunkel	Bronze
Wood/barrel-aged	Bronze
Belgian abbey ale	Bronze
American pale ale	Bronze
Belgian strong specialty ale	Gold
Belgian sour ale	Gold
Imperial stout	Gold
Wood/barrel-aged	Bronze
Belgian-style sour ale	Bronze
Smoke-flavored	Silver
German schwarzbier	Silver
German Schwarzbier	Bronze
German brown ale	Gold
American cream ale/lager	Gold
American premium lager	Gold
American cream ale/lager	Gold
American cream ale/lager	Gold
American specialty lager	Gold
American lager	Bronze
Experimental	Bronze
French/Belgian saison	Bronze
Belgian/French ale	Bronze
Baltic porter	Silver
French/Belgian saison	Gold
Strong Scotch ale	Bronze

*Defunct

PHILADELPHIA MEDALISTS

Year	Brewery	Beer
2000	New Road*	Perkiomen Pils
2002	Nodding Head	BoHo Pilsner
2002	Nodding Head	Grog
2003	Nodding Head	60 Shilling
2003	Nodding Head	Ich Bin Ein Berliner Weisse
2004	Nodding Head	Ich Bin Ein Berliner Weisse
2005	Nodding Head	George's Fault
2005	Nodding Head	Ich Bin Ein Berliner Weisse
2003	Ortlieb's*	Ortlieb's Select 69 Lager
2006	Rock Bottom King of Prussia	Schwarzbier
2007	Rock Bottom King of Prussia	Broad Street Barleywine
1998	Samuel Adams Brewhouse*	Cream Stout
2002	Sly Fox	French Creek Helles
2003	Sly Fox	Pikeland Pils
2007	Sly Fox	Pikeland Pils
2007	Sly Fox	Instigator
2001	Stewart's	Stewart's Smoked Porter
2003	Stewart's	Stewart's Oktoberfest
2003	Stewart's	Stewart's Barleywine
2007	Stewart's	Stewart's Oktoberfest
1988	Stoudt	Stoudt Gold
1989	Stoudt	Stoudt's Weizen

Style	Medal
German pilsener	Gold
Bohemian pilsener	Bronze
English brown ale	Gold
Scottish ale	Silver
German wheat ale	Silver
German wheat ale	Silver
Specialty honey lager/ale	Gold
German wheat ale	Bronze
European pilsener	Silver
German-style schwarzbier	Silver
Aged beer	Gold
Sweet stout	Gold
Munchner helles	Bronze
German pilsener	Bronze
German-style pilsener	Gold
German-style strong bock	Bronze
Smoke-flavored	Bronze
Marzen/Oktoberfest	Bronze
Old ale/Strong ale	Gold
German-style Marzen	Silver
European pilsener	Silver
Wheat	Gold

*Defunct

PHILADELPHIA MEDALISTS

Year	Brewery	Beer
1990	Stoudt	Bock Oktoberfest
1990	Stoudt	Dortmunder Export
1990	Stoudt	Stoudt's Weizen
1991	Stoudt	Doppelbock
1991	Stoudt	Oktoberfest Marzen
1991	Stoudt	Golden Lager
1992	Stoudt	Mai Bock
1992	Stoudt	Fest
1992	Stoudt	Export Gold
1992	Stoudt	Golden Lager
1993	Stoudt	Bock
1993	Stoudt	Pilsener
1994	Stoudt	Mai Bock
1994	Stoudt	Pilsener
1994	Stoudt	Export Gold
1995	Stoudt	Honey Double Mai-bock
1995	Stoudt	Stoudt's Pils
1996	Stoudt	Honey Double Mai-bock
1997	Stoudt	Stoudt's Pils
1999	Stoudt	Stoudt's Pils
2000	Stoudt	Stoudt's Fest
2004	Stoudt	Oktoberfest
2007	Stoudt	Stoudt's Ofest
2007	Stoudt	Stoudt's Weizen
2004	Triumph Princeton	Kellerbier
2004	Triumph Princeton	Rauchbier
2005	Triumph New Hope	Dunkel
2005	Triumph New Hope	Honey Wheat

Style	Medal
Bock	Gold
Export/specials	Silver
Weizen	Gold
Bock	Silver
Marzen/Oktoberfest	Gold
Munchner helles	Bronze
Bock	Silver
Marzen/Oktoberfest	Gold
Munchner helles	Gold
Munchner helles	Silver
Bock	Silver
European pilsener	Gold
Bock	Bronze
European pilsener	Gold
Munchner helles	Silver
Bock	Honorable mention
European pilsener	Bronze
Bock	Silver
Pilsener	Gold
German pilsener	Silver
Vienna lager	Bronze
German Marzen	Bronze
Vienna lager	Bronze
South German-style hefeweizen	Silver
Beer with yeast	Gold
Smoke-flavored	Silver
Munchner dunkel	Silver
American wheat beer	Gold

*Defunct

PHILADELPHIA MEDALISTS

Year	Brewery	Beer
2005	Triumph New Hope	German Pilsener
2005	Triumph Princeton	Czech Pilsener
2006	Troegs	Troegenator Double Bock
2007	Troegs	Troegenator Double Bock
1996	Valley Forge*	Imperial Stout
2007	Victory	Victory Festbier
2007	Victory	Prima Pils
1987	Yuengling	Yuengling Porter

Other honors

Year	Brewery	
1999	Lion Brewery	Mid-sized brewing company of the year; head brewer Leo Orlandini
2005	Iron Hill	Large brewpub of the year; director of brewing Mark Edelson

Style	Medal
German pilsener	Bronze
Bohemian pilsener	Silver
Bock	Silver
Bock	Gold
Strong ale	Gold
German-style Marzen	Gold
German-style pilsener	Silver
Porter	Bronze

*Defunct

Index of Beer Bars

Isn't a "beer bar" a redundancy? Not in this guidebook. Here are more than 250 local joints where you can get something better than Bud-MillerCoors (and BassHeinekenCorona). Ask for a local brew; check out the list of premium imports. Remember: Life is too short to drink lousy beer.

Every one of these places has a beer list that's worth a visit, bold-faced venues especially.

BEER NOTES

BEER NOTES

BEER NOTES

Joe Sixpack's Philly Beer Guide

BEER NOTES

OF RELATED INTEREST

The Philadelphia Inquirer Restaurant Guide

Craig LaBan

"Other critics nibble at his turf, but LaBan, as the restaurant arbiter for the region's newspaper of record, is the only one approaching make-or-break power...."

Noted restaurant critic Craig LaBan presents 76 in-depth reviews of favorites, in addition to over 600 capsule reviews of all the other enticing eateries in town—from the Delaware Valley to the Jersey Shore. Sensuous and authoritative, as the best food writing should be, LaBan's expert advice is also a pleasure to read.

The Philadelphia Inquirer's Walking Tours of Historic Philadelphia

Edward Colimore

Walk back in time as you take twelve tours through different city neighborhoods, visiting buildings, streets, gardens, and parks that remain testaments to Philadelphia's historic past. This is the definitive resource for visitors and residents alike who want to stand in the spot where William Penn first set foot in his new city, follow in the footsteps of Washington, Jefferson, and Franklin, and explore grand Victorian-era buildings that remain a vibrant part of life here.